LANCASHIRE

WITHIN LIVING MEMORY

Compiled by the Lancashire Federation
of Women's Institutes from contributions sent by
Institutes in the County

Published jointly by
Countryside Books, Newbury
and the LFWI, Preston

First published 1997
© Lancashire Federation of Women's Institutes 1997

COUNTRYSIDE BOOKS
3 Catherine Road
Newbury, Berkshire

ISBN 1 85306 467 X

Front cover photograph taken at Tarleton cotton mill
Christmas 1951, supplied by Beth Ross, Rufford WI.

Back cover photograph of sheep washing in the
Hodder river, supplied by Agnes Walker, Broughton WI.

Produced through MRM Associates Ltd., Reading
Printed by J. W. Arrowsmith Ltd., Bristol

CONTENTS

Lancashire

Lancaster

Fleetwood

Forest of Bowland

Blackpool

Lytham

Pendle Hill

Preston

Industrial Revolution

Southport

Ormskirk

Manchester

Liverpool

MLynskey

FOREWORD

Welcome to Old Lancashire. Walk back into recent history through the memories of WI members.

Our County is one of the most populated in Britain, but the sprawling busy urban areas around Manchester and Liverpool have total contrasts in peaceful little villages, country lanes and open moorland. From the long varied coast to the bleak heights of the Pennines, we can justly claim that this County has a little of everything.

In years gone by, the mainstays of employment were coal and textiles; over the last 30 years things have changed. A little of the more specialised textile industry lives on, but power now comes from the gas fields off our coast and not a single mine remains. New industries have taken over – aerospace, cars, plastics and food manufacture – but the greatest growth has been in tourism which helps to sustain the more rural areas, such as the picturesque Ribble Valley.

Lancastrians have always been people with very strong identity and this has been passed on to generations of immigrants into the County over the years: Irish from the 1800s, East Europeans during the Second World War and more recently Asians seeking a more prosperous future in the textile industry.

Lancashire has always worked hard and played hard but with a sense of humour and friendliness which cannot be bettered anywhere in Britain. Blackpool is still the playground of the north.

There is a sense of history, also a glint of humour and determination in the Loyal Toast always proposed in the County as 'The Queen, The Duke of Lancaster' which takes us back 500 years to the Wars of the Roses. This does not go down well with those rivals over the border in Yorkshire. To those who live further afield this County rivalry may seem slightly strange but it is surprisingly real. A recent survey by Leeds University confirmed, to the delight of Yorkshiremen, that squirrels in the White Rose County are a different race from those in Lancashire.

In this book you are treated to a unique collection of 'snapshots' of Lancashire life. My grateful thanks to Dorothy Ritchie who collected all the information to make this book possible.

Audrey Weatherill
County Chairman

ACKNOWLEDGEMENTS

The Lancashire Federation of Women's Institutes would like to thank the following for their help in the production of this book:-
Mary Lynskey. Weeton WI, for the drawing of the county map and the delightful illustrations throughout; members of staff at WI House for helping to type some of the copy; Maureen Gerrard, Thurnham WI, for her kind advice whenever needed; and last but by no means least the WI members from all over the county who searched their memories and sent in such a wide variety of interesting contributions. Unfortunately, because of the space available and to avoid duplication of content, not every entry has been used but each one was of great value and without them this book could not have been so successfully produced.

Dorothy Ritchie
Co-ordinator

TOWN & COUNTRY LIFE

M.Lynskey

SOME TOWNS AND VILLAGES REMEMBERED

Looking back over the 20th century, so much has changed in town and country within living memory – these are just a few snapshots of life in Lancashire as it was.

◈ SABDEN – THEN AND NOW ◈

'Sabden lies in the Ribble Valley at the foot of Pendle Hill. At the turn of the century it was a thriving, bustling cotton village with three mills – Cabden's, Stuttard's and The Company, where raw cotton was produced by winding, spinning and weaving, after which the cloth went to what was known as the top works for bleaching, and then to the bottom works for dyeing, printing and finishing.

The cloth was then taken away, in the early days by horse and cart and later by the mills' own lorries to the station at either Whalley or Simonstone, to be sold on the cotton market.

The mill owners built houses in the village for their workers and in the 1950s as many as three buses brought workers to the mills, mainly from Padiham, and then took them home at the end of the day. Work was from 5 am to 8.30 am, 9 am to 12.30 pm and 1.30 pm to 5.30 pm, village workers being summoned back to work by the factory whistle at 8.55 am and 1.25 pm.

Accidents often happened at the mills, with people getting their hands or clothing caught in the machines, or the shuttles flying out and hitting the workers, and fire was always a hazard because of the heat from the engines and all the fluff that used to stick to them. Some of the fires were minor and others, which destroyed parts of the buildings and machinery, were severe. Flooding was a particular problem, too. The mills were built on the side of the brook and you had to go down steps to the mill floor with the result that if we had torrential rain and the brook overflowed its banks the mills were flooded.

Sabden was a thriving cotton village in the 1900s, nestled at the foot of Pendle Hill. (Eileen Harrop – Sabden WI)

With the decline in the 1960s and 1970s of the cotton industry the mills closed one by one. Today there are no mills left. Some of the mill buildings have been demolished and those that remain have taken on a new lease of life as an antiques centre, a furniture manufacturing business, a paper printing business and small industrial units.

In the early 1900s the village had in excess of 25 shops and businesses, among them a post office, drapers, bakers, a selling-out shop, a large Co-op, and one shop that was like Aladdin's Cave; you could buy anything there from a pound of sugar to paraffin or a gas mantle.

We had our own village doctor and several cloggers, who made and repaired the clogs of the mill workers (most of the children, too, wore clogs during the week and only had shoes for Sunday best). Add to these the travelling tradesmen who came into the village like Hugills who sold hardware and ironmongery goods, the "fish and veg man", the haberdashery man from Read (just over the hill from Sabden) and the oatcake and muffin man. We must not forget too the local farmers who supplied and delivered milk twice a day, seven days a week. The milk was carried in a large can with a lid, the milk being ladled out with a ladling tin into the customers' own jugs. One of the milk deliverers, Clara Whitwell, did progress to a metal hand-cart, then to a motorised truck and finally to a van.

Sabden has four churches and all of them still play a large part in village life. The older members of the village remember things like the Baptist and Methodist "sermons" and gift weekends, when people turned out in their new clothes and hats – a real family occasion; Mothering Sunday when children presented their mums with posies of violets, daffodils, or biscuits; or Walking Days complete with banners and a band – two traditions the Anglican church still continues today. There were drama groups and Mothers' Union concerts, pantomines and harvest socials, and even classic films like *Oliver Twist* shown in the Baptist church schoolroom on a large screen. Many people went to church or chapel on Sunday morning and evening and to Sunday school as well if you were a child. Most of the churches ran extra activities like socials and dances, the Girls' Brigade, Girl Guides and Brownies, Boys' Brigade and Cubs, badminton clubs and billiards, choir contests and choir outings, some of which are still going. The baby clinic was run by two spinster sisters, a nurse and helpers for many years in the Methodist church schoolroom.

Sabden had good cricket teams and a brass band, which according to a newspaper report of a band concert in 1879 competed against Black Dyke Mills band and others and came second to Blackburn Borough Band, winning 20 shillings for doing so. The band continued well into the 1900s.

If there was nothing you fancied going to in the village then you could, if you could afford, go to the cinema in Padiham or Whalley but you had to walk in both directions, a distance of about seven miles in total. Later, with the advent of the motor car and buses, it was much easier to get about and go further afield.

The ladies of Sabden on Walking Day in the 1900s. (Eileen Harrop – Sabden WI)

On a Saturday afternoon if Burnley FC were playing at home, special buses were laid on to take village supporters to and from the match. On Saturday nights you could go by bus to the cinema in Burnley, Whalley or Clitheroe or dancing up the "Con Club" (Conservative Club), Accrington or the "Cems" (Assembly Rooms) in Whalley, but if you missed the last bus home at 11 pm (which we often did) then you had to get a taxi.

Most people now have cars (some more than one) so the bus service has declined and regular late night buses are gone, but you can still go down to one of the two remaining pubs in the village for a pint and a game of darts.

There are two thriving schools in the village, a Roman Catholic primary, and a County Primary opened in 1837 and founded by Richard Cabden, one of the mill owners, as well as a nursery school for age three to fives. In years gone by children started school at five years and left at 14 having had all their education at the same school. Nowadays children leave the village school at eleven years old to go to schools in neighbouring towns.

Everyone likes to celebrate and our village was no exception. There were village sports days and maypole dancing on May Day, rolling hard boiled eggs down Pendle Hill at Easter, and at Hallowe'en riders on horseback from the local riding school wearing fancy dress and carrying lanterns, riding on Pendle Hill, home of the Lancashire witches. The travelling fair came with merry-go-rounds and the coconut shy, and there was Mischief Night on 4th November, tying people's door snecks to the next door and then knocking on the doors and waiting round the corner, laughing whilst the owners tried to open their doors, and scrumping apples and pears and going home with tummy ache.

Sabden today is still a lovely village to live in, with plenty going on. It has its fair share of vandalism and car parking problems – what village hasn't? The main thing is the people are friendly and in the main helpful. It used to be said that you had to be born here in the village or have lived here for at least 30 years before you could be called a Sabdener. There are still people living in the village who were born here but a lot of people are outsiders who have come to live in the area and commute to work in the surrounding towns.

Our village has grown tremendously over the last 90 years but because of the green belt regulations very little building can take place nowadays.' *(Eileen Harrop – Sabden WI)*

▣ St Michael's, Gem of the Fylde ▣

'The river Wyre ford gave life to the charming village of St Michael's, named after the ancient parish church. Positioned in the beautiful Fylde countryside, it is approximately nine miles from Preston, Lancaster and Blackpool, hence the heavy traffic over the present bridge built in 1803. Many wooden bridges have spanned the river over the ages, the first stone bridge being built circa 1696. The longed-for by-pass, to restore peace, has yet again been shelved.

An uneasy co-habitation with the river has been endured for

centuries. Many times, in adverse weather conditions, the meandering waters have become swollen with torrents from fells upriver, where the Wyre is joined by the river Brook. Wide-scale flooding has occurred, badly affecting houses, farms and livestock, as banks burst or overflowed; October 1980 proved the last major incident. Much expensive work by the Water Authority has since avoided flooding, though tried to the limit in February 1995.

One life-long villager recalls as a child a flat-bottomed boat being deposited by a flood on the family's riverside farm. "We used it for fishing and catching snigs, then a later flood took it away." Snig is the colloquial name for eel. One method of catching them is called switching or clatting. This was achieved by threading worms on worsted and securing it to a stiff pole about seven feet long. On biting the worms the eels' teeth became entangled on the worsted and they were hauled out, sometimes several at once. An excellent food source, they were skinned and fried. Today the river is much changed and banks are built higher. For most village inhabitants, in those early days, life and work on the land was long, hard toil. In the Fylde area much land required draining, and bad weather and/or poor harvests all took their toll. Farm labourers worked until they could no longer support themselves in their tied cottages, then, with no pensions, it was the workhouse and parish relief. The work women had to undertake in the home was formidable, even for the strongest. In June women also worked in the fields, with fustian (twilled cotton cloth) wrapped around their knees, as they crawled around thinning turnips. They would also assist with the planting and harvesting of vegetables and potatoes, often heavy with child.

Many children had to walk two or three miles to school, often arriving soaked. Shoes and socks were dried by the school fire (the smell lingers on in memories!). Paper was scarce and expensive, used only by older pupils. When exercise books were filled, the children gave them to Dolly Smith in the village, in exchange for toffee. Dolly would then sell her home-made toffee wrapped in the paper!

In April, children were often kept from school to cut peat on

The children of St Michael's, in 1935 and in 1995. (Judith Hunter – St Michael's WI)

the moss, in June and July for haymaking and in August or September for blackberry picking. Even younger children would have to weed between the farmyard cobbles or paths around the house. On leaving school at twelve years old they often had to go into service, packing their few belongings in a wooden box when leaving home, in order to make room for their siblings. They would however learn "big house" skills, and these they would eventually pass on to their children.

When not working, children entertained themselves playing by the river on fallen trees or with skipping, rolling hoops and home-made whip and tops. Mischievousness was also around; tubs of water or bags of chaff were at times propped against doors and the householder, answering the knock, would end up with wet feet or a pile of chaff in the doorway! Chaff was also used for bedding inside a large tick, a large heavy cotton bag, though a donkey's breakfast (hay) was more usual.

In 1928 the matron of a Blackpool children's home retired and moved to St Michael's, along with her two sisters, both nurses and midwives. All their skills were put to good use and there are still local people who were delivered by one or the other of the Swallow sisters. At this time the Big Wheel in Blackpool, built in 1896, was being demolished and the 30 carriages auctioned; the matron bought one and had it positioned against the wall of her cottage, on the outskirts of the village. At nine feet by 29 feet this provided sleeping accommodation for children from the home who came to stay for their summer holidays. Each Sunday they were marched the one and a half miles to church and village children looked forward to having more friends to play with. Later the carriage was used as a tea room and is still in good condition today, 100 years after it was built, now being used as a conservatory.

Before septic tanks, which are still heavily relied on in this area, one trotted out back to the privy, often situated next to the family pigsty. It was a "bucket and chuck it" situation. With the large families of the day the old "two holer" saved valuable time, and at nearby Rawcliffe Hall, there was a *twelve seater*! Children were sent in pairs, at their allotted time; one local recollects the pairs never interchanged and his "time" is still the same in retirement! Sewers were finally laid in the village in the late 1970s.

Down the years tragedies have hit villagers and, apart from intermittent flooding, a more recent shocking tragedy occurred in May 1984, when a group of villagers were being shown the Water Authority's outfall station at Abbeystead, built to relieve flooding. A massive explosion occurred, killing 16 people and badly injuring many more. The church holds a plaque in memory of those who died.

St Michael's church is responsible for the upkeep of the excellent village school, a tradition centuries old. The present modern, airy building, opened in 1969, replaced the one some parents remember. There are many on and off site school activities and an active PTA. Social life today is probably more alive than in many larger towns, with a modern village hall complete with all facilities. Fishermen enjoy the lovely river and three fishing lakes, where large trout and carp can be caught. Enthusiasts of the local microlight aircraft school can often be seen flying over the village, no doubt enjoying the views.

The old poultry farms have made way for groups of sympathetically designed houses, tucked here and there in and around leafy lanes, their occupiers swelling the population of village and school. Everyone enjoys the annual gala and raft race and garden party held at the home of the Hornby family, whose forebears were vicars of St Michael's for 140 years.

And so the community goes forward with traditions old and new and for its courage in adverse times it has earned the name, locally, of "brave" St Michael's.' (*Judith Hunter – St Michael's WI*)

◼ HEYWOOD BETWEEN THE WARS ◼

'I was born in 1922 in Heywood, a town whose industry was mostly cotton mills of various kinds but which had views to the Pennines and large open areas and several farms. Our milk was brought to the house by the farmer or his wife who came in a horse and float, an open cart which held the large kits of milk. The farmer would tap on the door and walk in where a jug would be waiting on the table. Into this he would pour as much milk as you wanted after measuring it out in a pint measure and always put in a generous extra splash from the large can. They came morning and tea time every day all the year round, bringing untreated milk straight from the cow.

The long lane we went down to school had open land on both sides, one side being cultivated into allotments. In the summer people used to go there for two or three pennyworth of salad. They took a clean teacloth and would receive an assortment of young lettuce, cress, mint and spring onions, deliciously fresh, and perhaps buy a lovely bunch of sweetpeas for sixpence.

In winter we had, in addition, to heavy snowfalls, very severe thick fogs and coming home from school along the darkening lane was eerie and not a little unnerving. How reassuring were the lights which shone from the windows of a mill as we got nearer to it and the clanging of the tramcars' warning bell as we reached the main road.

Another great change has been the elimination of many of the diseases which were prolific when I was a child, especially diphtheria and scarlet fever. In the 1920s and 1930s during the months of November and December, especially, it was common to see the "fever" ambulance arrive and carry some poor unfortunate child off to Marland, which was the isolation hospital for the town. Although I fortunately didn't have this experience myself, an awful lot of children did and word quickly spread around that so-and-so had been taken to Marland.

Dawson's was a fair sized shop in Bury Street, with sacks of sugar, peas, beans, dog biscuits, chicken food, bran and flour standing all round the floor. Large boxes of dried fruit filled the shelves (all produce was weighed out as required in those days, no packaging to add to the cost) and on the top shelf stood large canisters lacquered in black and with the contents in gold lettering. Those filled with tea or coffee had an oriental design painted on them. They were really quite imposing.

A little further down the street was Hilton's (herbalists). I can picture the little man of very solemn appearance standing behind the counter attending to the needs of his customers amidst this haunting aroma of liquorice, aniseed, camphor, herbs and cough sweets. Many is the time I was sent there for a 3d box of marshmallow ointment. This (made by Mr Hilton himself) was taken from a large pot and a circular cardboard box was filled and the appropriate lid popped on (no screw tops or glass jars then).

In those far off days all the shops, or at least the tripe shop, the butchers, greengrocers and chip shops, had flagstone floors which were regularly swilled with hot water, containing washing soda, and brushed clean with the use of long handled, very stiff bristled brushes. When the floors were dry they were sprinkled with sawdust or fine sand which crunched when people wearing clogs walked on it.

In the town centre there was Hill's shop; it was known as a "temperance bar" and here you could buy hot or cold fruit cordials, tea, coffee, Horlicks, etc, besides sweets and chocolates. They also made potato pie, and pie and peas that could be consumed on the premises or taken away. The smell emanating from there on a chilly winter's evening was delicious.

Living as we did on the tramcar route, trams were prominent in our lives. There was one which used to come along from Bury every evening (except Sunday) that arrived at Wham Bar at 9 pm and on the back of it was a letter posting box, so if you missed the last collection (8 pm) from the Wham Bar postbox, you could wait for the tram and put your letter in the box on the back.

I remember too, when wireless was in its infancy. My father used to make his own wireless set, as did many other people. First it was a three valve, then four valves, and when it got to five valves we really were getting there. With my cousin I used to take the accumulator (which helped the wireless to work) to be recharged at the garage up the road. There was a special container with a handle in which we carried this thing. It would be left at the garage overnight and would be collected the next day.

Heywood being mostly a "Cotton Town" was very badly hit during the depression of the 1920s and 1930s. I can remember seeing long queues of people outside the Labour Exchange waiting to sign on. Various activities were organized to try to help people in need, during these lean years. Housewives were asked at Christmas time if they could make an extra Christmas pudding to give to someone out of work. I remember seeing all the puddings that had been donated, each one wrapped in white muslin cloth, hanging from a string in a shop window in the centre of the town opposite St Luke's church. On Christmas Eve the puddings were distributed throughout the town, and I suspect some people had little else but that on Christmas Day.

It was not uncommon in my childhood for a man or a woman to wander up and down the streets singing, in the hope that people would give them a copper or two (hence the saying, "Give him tuppence to go in the next street!"). Some of the singing was pretty awful. It was also quite common for people "on the road" to knock on your door and ask for money. Very often if they got it, it was quickly spent at the nearest pub. Also vying for the odd copper was the hurdy-gurdy man who came down the street playing his organ and the gypsies that came along selling their wooden pegs and wanting to tell your fortune.

It was during the "lean years" that the unemployed built the lake in Queens Park. My uncle was one of the people involved in building it. Many people will remember the pleasures of the park, the peacock enclosure, the band concerts on Sunday afternoons and evenings when people paraded around the bandstand, some to listen to the band, others to show off their new clothes and some to look out for a possible girl or boy friend. Those were the days when you could hire rowing boats, or ride on the motor launch.

During the annual Wakes Week when the town virtually closed down, many people went away, usually by train. On their return, either at Broadfield or Heywood stations, as they descended from the train they would be met by boys and men asking, "Carry your bag, mister?" and having completed the task, hoping to be suitably rewarded with sixpence or a shilling.

In the summer we would go to Whitings farm, at the Summit, to help with the haymaking. Those were golden days indeed, when it seemed that every day was sunny and hot, and the hay smelt lovely as we rode back from the field on the laden cart which "dripped" hay all the way along the lane. Small pleasures by today's standards, but very happy days.' (*Barbara Grace – Lytham Green WI*)

◻ THE SANDHILLS ◻

'In 1925 my parents moved to a house built on the heathland between St Anne's-on-Sea and Fairhaven. There were some bungalows nearby with a few shops but the skyline and the way to the shore was blocked by high sandhills, the tallest being higher than the bungalow roofs. We went beachcombing, and grown-ups carried home driftwood, broken fish boxes and anything useful while we picked up orange and green glass balls that had been markers for nets. Once the sea was dotted with grapefruit which littered the shore and came bobbing in with the tide. Everyone ran home for baskets and collected them but unfortunately they were too salty to eat.

To reach the shore we scrambled up the sandhills, slipping in the soft sand, or found an opening with a track of wooden railway sleepers along which the shrimpers drove their carts following the tide out. My little sister was always sorry for the horses who had to get their feet wet!

In 1927 we climbed the tallest sandhill with our parents and friends to watch the total eclipse of the sun on 29th June at 5.30 am. We each took pieces of smoked glass to look through. It went very cold and dark and a huge cloud of seabirds flew round and round the estuary before it went completely dark. When the sun came back we had a lovely summer's day.

These sandhills were taken away over a number of years because the sand blew in drifts over the coast road to Blackpool and stopped the trams running. Houses came to be built over the patches of heathland remaining, covering up the scrub willow, wild pansies, harebells and toadflax where we had picked whinberries and tried to catch the sand lizards.' *(Billie Andrews – Appley Bridge WI)*

◻ OVER WYRESDALE ◻

'Tarnbrook is a small hamlet of four houses and nestles below Tarnbrook Fell and Wardstone, the highest point in Lancashire, being 1,836 feet above sea level, and a green hill called Greenside in Over Wyresdale. It was this place where I was born. There were two farms and two cottages. Both farms were occupied by

Estate workers at Abbeystead collecting ice, 1903. In the background is the gamekeeper's cottage. (Catherine Tallentire – Abbeystead WI)

Pye families and the cottages were the homes of Lord Sefton's estate workers.

School was a three mile walk to Abbeystead, a long walk in all weathers for one so young. But it was a picturesque walk following the river Wyre, which has its source on Tarnbrook Fell and flows out at Knott End where a ferry is used daily to cross to the port of Fleetwood. In spring there were birds' nests to watch and wild flowers – primroses grew on two banks (alas, no more) and wild white hyacinths grew in one certain place. Tall alders grew on the river side, no doubt planted to preserve the river banks. Often it flowed placidly with dipper birds and sandpipers bobbing on the stones, but it could be a raging torrent in flood. Abbeystead school was built in 1674 and is still a fine building of local stone. It usually has 30 to 40 children attending, with an infants teacher and a headmaster, and until 1959 it was an all-age school. We had to take our own lunch each day; the kettle was boiled for cocoa in winter but not in summer.

Wyresdale church was four miles away and the Methodist chapel about two miles over fields, so I attended there for Sunday school at 1.15 pm followed by the service at 2 to 3 pm. Everyone had to walk as only about three farmers had cars then.

In 1926 King George V visited Abbeystead House as a guest at Lord Sefton's grouse shoot. I remember the day well when he rode past our house on a Norwegian pony. They dismounted a few yards away and drove off in beautiful shiny cars. The schoolmaster was always proud to think he had played the church organ in the presence of the King.

Farming in the 1930s was very hard work for small returns. Our house was dated "WGI 1730", a nice dry house but it had a blackleaded fireplace and stone floors. In winter we separated the milk and made butter in a hand-operated churn. In summer we made cheese. It was interesting work but washing the utensils and cloths was very hard work. The cheeses weighed 40 lbs each and were stored upstairs in a cheese room and turned every day. The cheese buyer came monthly from Preston and the price varied from 6d to 10d per pound.

The grocer from the nearest shop at Dolphinholme used to take them to a storehouse in Preston for us when he had delivered the groceries. He bought our butter and eggs himself and the price was usually 8d per pound. Eggs in spring were 8d per dozen. What a pleasure it was when the Milk Marketing Board started to buy the milk for cheese dairies; we had a monthly cheque all year round.

Sheep were our mainstay but I remember when the wool was sold for 4d per pound. The lambs were born in April and the sheep were sheared in June. The shearing was done communally with each farm having a fixed day and everyone went to help, which was a worry for the ladies if it had to be postponed because of the weather. It took a lot of food preparation to feed all who helped both inside and out.

Folk had to make their own entertainment. We had family parties in the winter, also concerts and dances in the school, Band of Hope meetings monthly for six months and in the summer there was the Field Day with a dance at night. In 1940 a committee was formed for a horticulture show which is still a

Abbeystead pupils in 1924. (Catherine Tallentire – Abbeystead WI)

huge success. Sometimes a day trip to the seaside or the Lake District was arranged and very much enjoyed.

The war years were hard in a different kind of way. My memories of Dunkirk are of very hot summer days when we were cutting peat on the fell and drying it in the hot sun. The first thing we did on returning home was switch on the wireless and listen to the wonderful but sad news of our soldiers' rescue from France. Our local lads all got home, though one had a leg wound, and another who was in the RAF was later killed flying home from Norway.

Then in 1941 the OCTU (Officer Cadets Training Unit) came for a three month training session, practising on our fell land. After that they came non-stop until late 1945. What made it hard was the fact that all our dogs and horses were terrified of gunfire and it was impossible to do any work with them, such was their terror. The soldiers' motor vehicles were parked near our house and their drivers had to wait all day for them to return. The ATS girls drove their officers and the ambulance so they were glad of a seat by our fire on cold days and we got friendly with most of them.

About 1880 the Earl of Sefton bought the area and built Abbeystead House. The most interesting thing about the building of the house, the lodges, Home Farm and the coachhouses was that the stone was quarried on the estate and dressed on the site, a quite outstanding undertaking when every load had to be moved by horse and cart from a quarry on Tarnbrook Fell. It stands on high ground facing south with beautiful landscaped gardens and woodland.

After Lady Sefton's death in 1980 the Duke of Westminster bought the estate and many improvements have been made, especially to the houses. Quite a lot have been sand-blasted and the stonework looks new. Tracks have been made on to the fells for the Land Rovers to use at the shoots and during heather burning. The Duke gives a party at Christmas to all his staff and tenants and they also have distinguished people to stay. Members of the Royal Family, including the Queen, stay on private visits because they like the quietness and serenity of our beautiful area.' *(Catherine Tallentire – Abbeystead WI)*

▨ THE SOUNDS OF ROCHDALE ▨

'The tall chimneys which dominated the Lancashire towns have almost disappeared and consequently the buildings and surrounding moors are now cleaner than at any time since before the Industrial Revolution. As a child raised between the wars I don't think the environment of smoking chimneys gave any lasting impression. I can only recall that summer days seemed endless – no coats worn for school for weeks – which was perhaps as well as most children had to wear almost the same clothes winter and summer. The winters were cold and the fogs black, but a good woollen scarf wrapped around the mouth and throat helped to keep out the worst as the dirt on the scarf testified. All this pales into insignificance when I remember the sounds of those days in Rochdale.

An alarm clock was a luxury few could afford but it wasn't difficult to know the time – early morning was not heralded by the birds but by the sound of the "knocker-up", a man who for a few pence a week would come along to your house with a long pole on which a small piece of metal was fixed, to knock on the bedroom window until a voice answered his call. Then came the sounds of the neighbours preparing for work, emptying their fire-grates and tipping the ashes into the bin, chopping sticks to set the fire ready for when they came home or for a neighbour to light later in the day for them. Then the first sounds of the clogs, a growing crescendo of noise as more and more workers set off to the mills. The mill whistles and hooters would sound, some deep and doleful, some light and shrill, but all warning the workers that they only had another few minutes to get to their places of work. The clogs hurried now and as the sound died away only a few stragglers remained, running to avoid being locked out, for this meant lost time and money.

Most of the mills started work early but engineering workshops and the like started a little later, so a further sound of heavy boots was now heard on the "flags" outside, a more measured tread than the clattering clogs, and a deep mutter of conversation between workmates. Walking to work was the rule for most people, no cars then.

Some like my father caught the train from the nearby station, so the sound of the trains – steam, of course – was always there, like a background to our daily lives. It gave us another way of knowing the time of day: the 7.15 am which went all the way to Manchester, the twelve o'clock which heralded dinner-time, the 5.45 which meant Dad was returning home, the 9.10 which meant you should be asleep, or the shunting of the coal wagons which kept you awake.

Coal, the life-blood of those days, was brought in wagons to the local station and shunted into the sidings where coal merchants collected it for bagging. Several coal-men came round the area each week with a horse and cart. Huge horses, they seemed – the pride of their owners, but the steady clomp of their hooves on the paved streets did not seem to match their size, it almost appeared they refrained from giving full vent to the strength in their legs for fear of damaging the road. The price of cobs, slack and nuts was of paramount importance and the sound of the coal being tipped down the cellar grate seemed to shake the foundations of the house. No sooner had the coal-man left than out came the sweeping brush and every scrap was swept down the cellar grate. Then out would come a bucket of water, scrubbing brush and cloth – the flags must be cleaned. The constant battle raged by housewives against dirt was almost unbelievable.

The dinner-time hooters preceded the return of the mill workers to their homes for a midday meal, so again the clatter of clogs, to be followed by half an hour of quietness while food and a short rest were taken. No rest for the women though, they had jobs to do, maybe a quick trip to the corner shop or to a neighbour to ask them to watch their washing and take it in should it rain.

Tradesmen always called their wares, shouting "Coal" or "Milk" or whatever. Paper boys called out the name of the paper they carried, such as "Football Final" or on Saturdays, "Green Final" which was a local rag giving cricket scores in the summer and football scores in the winter. Rag and bone men were abundant, and the cry of "Rags" was heard many times a day.

Quite often in those days, before many people even had a radio or gramophone, the only music heard was played by local bands (mostly brass or silver) formed by groups of workers, the Salvation Army, or as in our area, a band from the local Catholic orphanage. The Boys' Brigade bands were usually most enjoyed, especially when the leader was expert in throwing his staff up in the air and catching it, performing all the usual twists and turns whilst we children stood waiting for him to drop it at the crucial moment (he never did while I watched anyway).

Occasionally self-taught musicians appeared in the street, squeaking out unrecognisable tunes on violins – not begging of course, that was against the law, but always hoping someone would offer the odd copper. The saddest sounds were the street singers, usually fairly old men and women who walked the streets singing songs and holding out their hands for money if anyone walked by; they always seemed to sing sad songs but I suppose their hard life did not encourage a happy frame of mind. I must have been impressed by them for my mother often told the story of one day finding me walking in the gutter down the street singing in a like manner, for which I was duly chastised.

At four o'clock school was over for the day and the sounds of children at play could be heard. The street seemed to divide itself as far as the children were concerned, those in the top third formed one gang, those in the middle another and those at the bottom end were rarely seen apart from Bonfire Night when a gradual joining of resources made sure ours was the biggest bonfire in the area, or so we thought.

At five thirty came the return of the workers and their slower gait showed the extent to which their daily labour had exhausted them – their clogs gave a slower measured clatter in contrast to the quick tapping in the morning. For an hour after tea we were allowed, if it was light enough or fine weather, a further period of play – different games in the twilight, with pieces of string known as burning bant lit surreptitiously from someone's fire and passed on so that all had a piece smouldering and showing a faint glow. Cries of "Jack, Jack, show your light" meant a swing of the smouldering string would arch a circle of light or twist in a figure of eight or other secret sign which let your playmates know where you were, all very exciting then. The sound of Father's whistle produced by putting two fingers in his mouth and blowing meant that our day was almost over and apart from the occasional sound of neighbours talking at their doors, quietness came with the night.' *(Greta Shepherd – Hornby WI)*

▣ BANKS VILLAGE ▣

'Banks has a population of about 3,500 now, but there were not so many in former years when we were known as North Meols, which historians tell us meant "northern sand dunes". Banks was always a fishing village, where the men made their living out of catching shrimps and cockles. Some of the women went with them to get cockles and all the wives helped to boil and shell the shrimps and then potted them in butter and took them to the shops and markets to be sold. A lot of the wives also sold home-grown produce at the markets in the mill towns. In those days we had a train service from Southport to Preston, which was very handy for people going out of the village to work. However, this was closed down in 1964 and houses have now been built where the station used to be.

About 150 years ago, it is said, a pirate ship went aground where the men used to fish and the fishermen, thinking it had been deserted, went to have a look around. However, they were wrong and to avoid being identified they called each other by peculiar names. These nicknames stuck with them for the rest of their lives and even today their families still carry on with them. There have been some embarrassing moments when strangers have come to the village and spoken to people, not knowing their proper names.

Banks Brass Band (then known as Banks Temperance Band) was formed in 1875 and is still going strong with most of its members from the village. Some families have two or three people in the band, perhaps the third or fourth generation to belong.

Banks was known at one time as "The Dry Village" as we had no public house. Then in the 1960s a farmhouse in the centre of the village was sold to the brewery and became the Fleetwood House Hotel. There was also a lovely mansion house in Banks called Greaves Hall, where Lord and Lady Scarisbrick lived for many years. During the Second World War it was opened as a hospital for people evacuated from Liverpool.

We have a Methodist church and school and St Stephen's parish church and school. Both of these have had their centenary. The crowning of the Rose Queen at the Methodist school, an annual event, used to be a great day. All the village turned out. The Queen and her attendants sat on the platform while the older girls, all in white and carrying roses, danced on the field. The younger children danced around the maypole and did other country dances in traditional costume. This finished when the war started in 1939. The Sunday school walking days were great days as well when, headed by the brass band and the Sunday school banner, we walked all round the village. There was tea in the school afterwards and then sports on the field, and the older folk would sit and listen to the band until dusk.

Another highlight of the summer was to take a picnic to the embankment when it was high tide. Dozens of people used to go and sit on top of the bank and watch the tide come up. Great days.' *(Jean Rimmer – Banks WI)*

▣ A SATURDAY IN ORMSKIRK 1936 ▣

'As winter dug its heels in with its accompanying bleak weather, the world of 1936 looked grey and forbidding for the 13 year old boy as he trudged from Tower Hill down Wigan Road to Ormskirk Market.

It was late Saturday afternoon in December. It had poured with rain all day but had eased somewhat leaving the pavements polished and the gutters awash with miniature torrents, dammed in places by Star, Woodbine and De Reske cigarette packets, held together with the dung of horses drained off the road.

On his left "the workhouse" with lights at every window without curtains, without movement, like a great liner with square port holes, going nowhere, anchored forever. Coming up the road towards him a myriad of lights, cycles with bright lights, dim lights bobbing and weaving their way to port, the steady twin candlelit lamps of a horse-drawn bread van plodding its way home at the close of a working day.

He passed the sawmill on his right. The aroma of new timber lingered in the night air, on his left the rope works where the man stood on the pavement, a rope spinning from the gloom of the works and fastened to his waist, where as it spun, he was gradually drawn into the gloom and vanished.

As he reached the Institute between Stanley Street and Beaconsfield monuments, he reflected on the scenes he'd witnessed there. Ladies in long sequined dresses, their partners in evening suits, going to dances; workers clattering up the stone steps when boxing or wrestling was held there. Of course, the Green and Red buses started from there, Ribble and Cadmans, going to far away places like Wigan, Southport, Skem and Bosca, the windows steamed up and slashed by fingers for seeing through, all in line patiently waiting their turn to get under way.

Ahead, towering above the main artery of Ormskirk, stood the Lord Beaconsfield monument, the silent sentry. As he moved onto the Moor Street Bridge the boy was suddenly enveloped with smoke, as a steam train belched its way out of Ormskirk station. As it emerged on the other side of the bridge the night sky was split with a red ribbon of light from its fire.

He crossed the road to the fringe of the market, where orange boxes lay broken and empty, and paper from them stuck to the pavement. The man on the stall shouted his prices to the night sky. The smell of apples, oranges and a variety of fruit was mixed with a whiff of paraffin from the light of the burner, which spluttered and coughed, and cast an eerie light.

As the boy drifted towards the Clock Tower people still lingered at the stalls, each stall having its own section, and each section its own identity: different coloured cheese on one stall; bacon laid on trays on another, with a pig's head as the centrepiece, an orange in the pig's mouth; glassy-eyed fish laid in rows, staring at nothing, their last resting place; and passing Jim Smith's chips and fish shop the appetising aroma of frying.

Colours, smells, shouts accompanied him to the Clock Tower where he looked up at the clock. It was 5.30 pm and he'd 1/6d from his morning paper round. It was Saturday, so he decided to go to the cinema.

He walked up Church Street, and over errand boys' cycles leant against shop fronts he glanced into the windows. Items were being withdrawn from the display, butcher boys were scrubbing down, men dashing into newsagents for the football paper.

He reached the Regal cinema, where coloured neon lights traced patterns on the walls and the front of the foyer. He paid his 6d at the kiosk, and felt he'd entered a royal palace; it was luxurious, warm, scented and of all things, the floor had a rubber surface. The lights dimmed and then went out; it was dark again.' *(Denis Crombleholme)*

◼ LONGRIDGE IN THE SNOW ◼

'As I think back over the 46 years I lived at a roadside farm, my most vivid memories are of the great snowfall in 1940. Longridge was cut off from Preston, so deep were the snowdrifts. We had a milk delivery round in Preston. Eight men pushed whilst my husband drove our empty milk van up the hill (Langton Brow) into Longridge. Then we hitched a door to our horse to make a large toboggan and took the milk into Longridge to transfer it to the van. This was repeated both going and returning home for about a week. After two days a large Riding's waggon got through to Preston round by the parish church, with my husband following it. Even so, two customers sacked us for not delivering their milk the previous two days!

The next farm to us was down a drive and it took six men six days to dig a road through. Doctor Binnie had to be tobogganed over all the hedges as the snow was so deep, to deliver a pregnant lady of her child down Hothersall Lane.

All the farmers were desperate as no one could collect their milk; then after a few days it was announced on the radio that any dairy would accept milk from any farmer providing he could get it there. As I washed up in our dairy that morning, the window looked over a long stretch of main road and what a wonderful sight it was; one after another came farmers taking their milk to Longridge dairy to be made into cheese. All had doors as sledges, full of milk churns, being drawn by horses.'
(Nellie Redmayne – Longridge WI)

THE FLOODS OF 1967

There have been many storms, snows and floods to recall over the years. The floods of 1967 brought danger and distress to these eye-witnesses.

▨ WRAY FLOOD ▨

'William and Alice Brown farmed Backsbottom, set deep in a gorge section of the Roeburndale valley, near Wray. This is Alice's personal account of their experiences during Wray flood, 8th August 1967.

"The 8th August 1967 was the day we had fixed for our annual dipping of ewes and lambs. Dipping was finished around 4.30 pm. A neighbour, Len Richardson from Stauvin Farm, two miles up the dale, came to help my husband, Bill. It was obvious that a storm was brewing. The sky was black but the horizon was so limited at Backsbottom, deep in Roeburndale valley, we did not see the full extent.

"Just after five o'clock, we decided to go into the house for tea. Torrential rain began with such a force that the river flooded the garden. 'We'd better get those sheep out of the pens,' said Len, and went out of the back door. Bill went out of the side door; Len opened the gate by the bridge and the ewes went through. By this time, the pen wall had collapsed and water was pouring through, washing back the lambs. They managed to get a few out, then the pressure of water washed the pen walls away; lambs were rolled over and over by the water – a sickening sight.

"I shouted to the men from upstairs; Len leaped to the other side of the river, and Bill dashed into the house. We saw the bridge go, just as if a bomb was under it. The water entered the house and rose up the stairs, and we decided to see the flood out in the end bedroom, at the higher end of the house. The doors of the van in the yard burst open under water pressure, the milk kits shot out and the van went with the current. A trailer was swept away. Our family of cats darted to and fro on the implement shed roof – then a crack – and the whole shed vanished. There was a great roaring; big trees, fully grown, were swept away; downstairs windows were being smashed.

"The house seemed to shake every second, as it was struck by trees and rocks. Realising that the house could not stand much more, and we were in the hands of providence, we clung together.

"After some time we could sense that the crashing against the house was less fierce. Looking to the meadow, we could see more of the hay-making machine, and realised that the water was falling slowly.

"Three youths suddenly emerged from the woods, shouting that help was on the way. Our son, Richard came running down the other side of the valley, looking terrified.

Men from Bentham Fire Brigade arrived, and after several

attempts to cross a deep channel in front of the house, finally reached us; we were helped down from the landing, the stairs having gone.

"The time was then 8.30, or 8.45 pm. We were worried about Len, but after leaving the sheep pens he had just got over the bridge before it went. We stayed overnight at Stauvins Farm. The milk cows were rounded up and taken to Allcocks Farm and Back Farm to be milked.

"Very little was left at Backsbottom Farm. All the barns and shippons, the stable, sheds and pig sty, and one end of the house had gone. So had all the farm machinery and equipment. Livestock losses were: one pig, one calf, two dozen hens, 45 lambs, one sheep, one of our dogs, all our cats, and the new-calved heifer and her calf."

'Alice Kenyon and her husband Richard lived in Main Street, Wray. "I remember the 8th August 1967 as being heavy and sultry all day. My daughter and her new-born baby girl were staying with us, and I was rather busy. Clouds began to build up, and it was black – so black.

"I was making rissoles for dinner – about 5.30 pm – when June Swindlehurst called to Dick, my husband, to say that the river was rising rapidly at the back of her house, which was opposite ours. He went to see, and as she brought the children over to us the river poured into her kitchen and downstairs rooms.

"We heard a great roar as the river surged up the lower part of Main Street. The bridge became jammed with huge trees, and boulders that had been ripped from the bed near the quarry, higher upstream. These had blocked the bridge, diverting water up the street. The timber and boulders smashed into the base of the lower houses, tearing out the walls of houses which had stood for two centuries or more.

"Dick, Gerry Forrest the policeman, and Roy Dixon managed to get Mr and Mrs Johnson out from their landing, by putting planks up and helping them down. Mrs Ruth Whittaker waded, chest-high, and broke through a downstairs window to get out of her house. She then managed to get her neighbours out, and they made their way up the gardens at the back to safety. Mr and Mrs

The destruction wrought in Wray by the floods of 1967.
(Cynthia Field – Wennington & District WI)

Bastow were rescued by planks, and her mother was wheeled in a wheelbarrow over the gardens, at the back, to the vicarage.

"Altogether, 13 houses near Bridge End were pulverised. Water rose to 25 feet above the river bed. No one could get through at the height of the flood. The roads were blocked; Meal Bank bridge at Wennington Road was down, and the telephone lines were cut.

"People were helping each other, taking shelter in the houses higher up Main Street, and being comforted. WVS ladies helped to prepare food for the dispossessed in Wray Institute. Dick and I went up to the Institute, taking tinned soup, bread etc, and other people brought tea and sugar to make warm drinks.

"First on the scene were the Bentham Fire Brigade. The next day, everyone helped to clear up the debris, and rescue what furniture and carpets and effects they could. Later, caravans were brought in to rehouse people who had lost their homes. The WVS continued to serve meals and distribute clothing in the meantime. Eventually, bungalows and houses were built for the people who had lost their homes. Little sign of damage appears today; but a flood mark and date – August 1967 – on the bus shelter in lower Main Street, commemorates that day."' *(Wennington & District WI)*

▓ On the Banks of the Hodder ▓

'It was a warm, muggy day, which I spent in our small market garden, hoeing and de-shooting the tomato plants in the Dutch Light House. In the distance thunder rumbled, in the background a yellow hue in the sky over Totteridge Fell.

My husband and I and our four sons lived in a cottage on the bank of the Hodder river. Opposite, the river Dunsop joined the Hodder, a short fast stream. Only one son was at home and it was about 3.45 pm when it started to rain. The skies opened; at times it seemed to be solid water coming down.

The rain went on for three quarters of an hour and then ceased. I went out onto the river bank to see if there was a flood; the Hodder and the Dunsop were slightly higher in level but nothing serious. It was then I looked towards the playing field, over the Newton/Dunsop Bridge road. A wall of water many feet high with complete trees upright in the water, floating along, was coming at some speed.

A fast retreat to the cottage, all hands on deck to close doors. We had a roadside stall on which we sold home-made jam amongst other goods. The sugar! Jack and I lifted hundredweight sacks onto stools to keep it dry. Ralph, meanwhile, was struggling with the front door. The weight of water burst the catch but he managed to get it fastened again. A gas cylinder floated by, the water was coming up the drains with the height of the water in the river. All the time we were lifting the sugar higher. As it turned out sugar occupied the whole of our time, nothing else was rescued, all we kept thinking was what a sticky mess there would be if the sugar got wet, the house would be all sticky.

In the midst of all the chaos, we remembered Laddy, David's dog. Laddy was blind; he was housed in the backyard in an old pig pen with stone walls. We went to bring him in but the water was too high. From then on Laddy occupied our minds.

There was nothing to do but wait until the water subsided. About 6.45 to 7 pm the water had gone down from the house and yard. Laddy, we found, had climbed up a piece of timber and was safe. The hens' building was wet, but they were dry in themselves. In the cottage everything was covered in mud and water to a depth of about three feet.

On emerging we all went on to the bridge to view the chaos. The Hodder was reasonable in height, if that had been in full flood we would have been in worse trouble.

Peter, our youngest son, had, while this was going on, been up at Woodend Farm. He had taken a circular walk and crossed a water pipe bridge to arrive in our yard safely. Eventually he came to us on the bridge. Peter just said, "Oh, there you are," and never spoke again for three days. We assume, I think rightly, he found the cottage empty, full of chaos and thought the worst, poor Peter.

A walk down the river bank was a shock; that was where behind a wall, perhaps 70 yards long, was what had been our market garden. One greenhouse was demolished, the other pushed partly over. The whole of the wall was flat and the plants gone.

The electricity was off and remained so for several days. There was no drinking water, the pipes had gone, and no chair to sit on, only stools. We found it a great hardship not being able to rest our legs as the days went on.

We all got up at 5 am the next morning and walked down the drive, on to the road and into Dunsop Bridge. There wasn't a sound, no birds, no animals, just a frightening silence.

Now the work began, we didn't know where to begin. Jack started on his wood and machines. The boys and I started taking out the ruined settee and easy chairs, carpet and lino from the kitchen, coats, wellingtons and shoes, the wireless! All were soaked and covered in mud, some wellingtons were missing. We never thought about the car, it must have floated then sunk.

The road to Brennand and Whitendale had been completely washed away in places. No way to Bishops House either. Holmehead looked battered, there the cottages are only a few yards from the Dunsop river.

The third day a man started stealing goods out of the yard, the wireless was taken. What an argument. He claimed we had abandoned the goods because we had put them outside. At Holmehead pinching was rife.

The local Member of Parliament came to view the scene. He told us to sell some of our possessions, for example the grandfather clock, as we had no money and were not able to claim from the DSS as we were self-employed.

Next came the insurance assessor. He put pairs of wellingtons together, "quite wearable," he said. (Odd sizes, please note.) The settee and chairs quite usable. We told him to sit on them and on it went. We were not insured for flood for many goods. All the photographs of the children growing up and of our wedding were lost. The smell had started by now, mouldy and disgusting. It takes time to get round to every cupboard and drawer.

We got cleaned up eventually but the walls were coated with black mould. Then we were offered a small shop in Slaidburn, followed by a house and finally a bigger shop, which we called "The Jampot".

Thank you to those who gave us furniture, to Mrs Laycock for the marvellous date loaf, the dairy kit of drinking water, and finally to the NFU for a small cheque to help us get going again.'
(Mary Bolton – Slaidburn WI)

BORN IN LANCASHIRE

Changes in county boundaries have led to many who are proud Lancastrians finding themselves cut off from their roots.

⬛ CHOPPED UP AND PARCELLED OFF ⬛

'I was born in Lancashire when it stretched from Morecambe to Manchester, Furness to Formby and right down at the bottom, to Widnes. We Widnesians didn't wear clogs and shawls or work in mills. The industry was chemicals, dominated by the giant ICI. The town had grown up from a collection of villages into a town of 50,000 people. Not so many of us could say that our grandparents had been born there but, wherever they came from, we lived in Widnes and that was Lancashire.

We had a lot to put up with in those days. Wherever we went and were asked what our home town was, we usually took a ribbing about the smell. I suppose there may have been a few noxious vapours wafting from the dozens of smoking chimneys but that was an accepted part of our industry. We were very proud of the high standing of ICI in the national economy. When ICI was doing well. Britain was doing well. Well, that was what we thought and I'm not sure it wasn't true.

What I liked about the chimneys was trying to read what the smoke was writing. We had a swing in the garden which faced south, towards the industrial part of the town, down by the river. The chimneys were lined up and all smoking. I don't ever remember making out any real words, and then the Clean Air Acts robbed us of the billowing plumes, blown east by the prevailing wind. I swung for many a half hour hoping for a word. Perhaps it was that the smoke blew from right to left and therefore backward.

We were also the proud owners of a rather unusual bridge. It was the Widnes Transporter Bridge which ferried passengers and cars across the river Mersey to Runcorn, Cheshire. It was one of only three in the country – the best, naturally. The bridge had a platform, known as The Car, suspended from a trolley which ran from one side of the bridge to the other. First it crossed the Mersey, which is sometimes hardly more than an expanse of sand and mud with a few wandering channels of water. This has proved a lifesaver; when an American serviceman, based at Burtonwood, hadn't grasped the idea of the bridge and drove through the closed gates, his car landed on the mud below.

The Transporter Car then crossed "the wall" and passed over the Manchester Ship Canal. At this point the canal runs directly alongside the river. We always hoped that there would be an ocean-going ship passing as we clank, clank, clanked forward. In summer there was often a gang of boys bathing in the canal. Having swum across the canal to the wall, they would climb on to it (in my memory it was eight or ten feet wide) using it as a lido. Sometimes a brave soul would jump up, grab the Transporter Car and drop off into the canal.

The Transporter Bridge was like a huge Meccano construction and it contrasted amazingly with the huge railway bridge which brought the London trains to Liverpool. This was built on massive sandstone pillars with cast ironwork girders in a diamond lattice pattern on each side. The footpath running along the outside reminds me of the Roman walls at York and Chester. As the path passes a pillar it has to skirt it, like a guard post.

We occasionally had to use the footpath on the railway bridge. Sometimes we went over into the green lanes and fields of Cheshire. People over there saw themselves as a cut above industrialised Lancastrians. If we arrived at the Transporter Bridge late in the evening we were in for a walk. The buses might be running on both sides but the Transporter only ran in the day and early evening. Maybe we had had a day out in Chester with the Youth Club, and a bit of bad timing was even built in to our return. The walk was the last bit of fun of the day, especially if

A view from the top of the Transporter Bridge, on the Widnes side, showing *supports. (Margaret Page – Longton WI)*

there was a good group of boys and girls. There were plenty of places where a couple of lads could hide and bob out to give the girls a scare. It was especially exciting if a train thundered across, flashing past at the other side of the latticed girders, belching egg sandwich-smelling smoke.

Alas, nothing stays the same. It was finally decided that there must be a road bridge across the Mersey at Widnes. Some people didn't feel that it was appropriate to have to drive up river to Warrington, to get across at night, or to queue for hours on busy days. It hadn't been so bad when hardly anyone had cars. As the barrier dropped and the gates swung open there might be a cabin full of foot passengers and only a few cars waiting.

Where would they build the new bridge? In the space between

hes of the railway bridge and below it, to the right, the base of the New Bridge

the two existing bridges, of course. It rose like a giant coat hanger, a baby Sydney Harbour Bridge. We were now becoming very proud of that, until we realised that it was usually called the Runcorn Bridge. What was happening to us? We really didn't see the need to be joined to the south by road. Cheshire had always been the next thing to abroad. We only went there on days out.

And then the final blow fell. They told us that now, not only were we to be joined by road to Cheshire but that we were to become part of it. I don't remember anyone asking me what I felt about Local Government Boundary Changes. Like so many other parts of England we were chopped off and parcelled up with people who were strangers.

If you go to Widnes now you will find that it is only part of

Halton, Cheshire and even ICI has moved over to Runcorn. The Transporter is long gone and the New Bridge is proving to be a bottle neck. The green fields of Cheshire seem to be covered by more and more roads, while I must say, Widnes is much cleaner and greener.' *(Margaret Page – Longton WI)*

CHURCH AND CHAPEL

Once Sunday was a day set apart from the hard work of the week, and many people can recall a time when Sunday school and church or chapel services were at the heart of our social life.

❖ NEVER ON SUNDAY ❖

'Hats were *always* worn by ladies for church. At Hoole between the wars we were not allowed to spend any money (apart from the church collection) on Sunday, not even bus fare, as this was causing somebody to work. Knitting and sewing were forbidden. Only the absolutely necessary work was allowed to be done in the home and on the farm.' *(Mona Lewis – Hoole WI)*

'We went to church in the morning, Sunday school in the afternoon and church again in the evening when I was growing up at Ramsbottom. We never went to church without some cover on our heads. We never played with skipping ropes or balls on a Sunday. We went for walks in our Sunday best, these clothes being kept specially for Sunday, and changed after church to keep them clean.' *(Beatrice Sellers – Greenmount Village WI)*

❖ SUNDAY AT GRANDMA'S ❖

'In 1934 there were four rows of two up, two down terraced houses carved out of the fields behind the Roe Lee Mills in Blackburn. I was born in one of them, my grandparents' home. There was no front street, just a row of flags and then a garden which to my memory is always full of sunshine, marguerites, old fashioned Dorothy Perkins rambling roses and sweet smelling pinks. Everyone in the family worked in the cotton mill.

Even when my parents moved to their own house all the family still returned "home" for Sunday tea. The best china and tablecloth were used, and we played cards or dominoes. At three o'clock we would hear a whistle and run to the top of the street where Baron's ice cream cart, pulled by a donkey, was waiting. There was no choice in those days, cornets for the children and wafers for the adults.

My grandfather was the bandmaster at the Queen's Hall. My uncle played the trombone and my cousins, both boys, played the cornet (girls were not allowed to play in the band). They practised every Sunday afternoon. I bet the neighbours hated it. My grandmother would take me to evensong and we walked over the fields to church. When we go back it would be time to catch the tram home.

That was our life until the war ended. By then we grandchildren were older and did not want to spend Sunday that way – and perhaps our grandparents were ready for some peace too!' (*Pat Keightley – Hapton WI*)

'During my primary school years in the 1950s Sunday usually began with Mass at 8 am, in my best clothes of course. Then I went back to Grandma's house for the day.

Sundays were always the same at Grandma's. Grandad would be sitting in the dining room, a small kindly old man who seemed to say little but who simply sat and watched the goings on of the women in the house. He was the only person I knew then who wore collarless shirts and his generous trousers were held up with a large buckled belt. The smell of pipe smoke filled the dining room and seemed to make it his own personal territory. I never remember seeing him in the kitchen, except when he was shaving with a magic, folding razor. The kitchen, after all, was a woman's place and this was where Grandma dominated the house.

She was rarely more than a few feet away from the Aga cooker, usually sitting on a hard-backed chair with a small black well-fingered prayer book in her hands. She was not given to unnecessary conversation and even less to idle chatter. Indeed, she had a steely eye that could pierce you at 100 paces and a tongue that could cut the atmosphere in half. She could chastise you as only an Irish woman could.

Back from church then, I would be allowed to help two maiden aunts. Aunt Sheila would always be baking, so I usually chose to sift the flour or grease the tins or stir the yeast for the bread rolls. She always made the same things. Queen of Puddings for after Sunday lunch, sponge cake and apple pie for tea and finger bread rolls.

Lunch was always at the large round table in the dining room, on blue and white willow patterned plates. Afterwards I would help my aunts dry the dishes in the tiny scullery. Sometimes Grandma would have visitors, usually another aunt or uncle with their children, my cousins. Visitors never came empty handed. It would be a tin of cold meat, some scones or another cake for tea. Sunday tea was always cold meat and salad. There would be celery standing tall in the cut glass jug and a large bottle of salad cream, something we never had at home, probably as it was a luxury. Children were, of course, seen and definitely not heard at the tea table, which was a quiet, civilised affair.

After tea it was time for church again. Benediction was 6.30 pm. I enjoyed this far more than Mass in the morning, not that I ever admitted this. There was never any singing at Mass and back then it was all in Latin. Benediction, on the other hand, included lots of familiar hymns and although many of these were also in Latin I knew them by heart. I always thought the priest's vestments were much more decorative at Benediction; it was a much brighter service altogether. This marked the end of my Sunday at Grandma's.' (*Jacqueline Wood – Dunsop Bridge WI*)

▨ THE LEYLAND CHURCH YEAR ▨

'We moved to Leyland in 1930 when my father was appointed minister of the Methodist church on Turpin Green. In those days Leyland was dominated by Leyland Motors. I was only three years old at the time, but have some vivid memories of life there.

The ministers of Leyland head the Walking Day procession, in top hats and frock coats. (Monica Chesworth – Over Kellet WI)

The church was a large galleried structure which has since been replaced by a smaller modern building. It boasted a large Sunday school, together with Boys' Brigade, Guide company, and Brownie pack. I was allowed to join the Brownies at an early age. A panama hat was part of our uniform, and I remember having difficulty in distinguishing between my left and right hand when required to give the Brownie salute.

One of the highlights of the Church Year was The Sermons, or Sunday school Anniversary when a large platform was built at the front of the church for a dramatic presentation by the children. Each year there was a different theme; I recall one year the older children building the city of Jerusalem from wooden blocks, and one of the older girls singing *The Holy City* from the walls of the city. I remember wondering whether they would collapse under her weight!

The At Home was a strange name for a three-day bazaar held at the church during the winter. Not only were there stalls and side-shows, but a concert each evening followed by a pie and chip supper. I well remember watching with envy the chorus line of older girls kicking their legs in the air and singing *All the nice girls love a sailor*. I had to be content with a paper bag of parched peas to eat during the performance.

Another highlight was Walking Day when we processed through the village headed by the ministers of the area in their top hats and frock coats. It was a great privilege to be a flower girl walking under the Sunday school banner. We took part in a similar procession at the May festival, a village event when the May Queen was crowned. On this occasion we ended up at Worden Park for sports and games. It was at such an event that a kind friend bought me my first packet of Smith's potato crisps costing two pence.' *(Monica Chesworth – Over Kellet WI)*

▣ SUNDAY SCHOOL AT BOLTON-LE-SANDS ▣

'In the 1920s I was a member of the Church of England at Bolton-le-Sands, going to Sunday school. On Ascension Day we went to church in the morning and in the afternoon we enjoyed games in the vicarage garden. The organist, Mr Hodgson, had his telescope set up on the church tower. At intervals a small party of us went up the spiral staircase, visited the belfry and heard the clock chime (a deafening noise), then went up to the top of the tower to see through the telescope over Morecambe Bay and the Lake hills.

We had a Sunday school outing each year and one year we had a trip on the canal in a horse-drawn coal barge which had been cleaned out and forms placed inside.

Just beyond Carnforth we alighted and went over a bridge to a field where we had tea and games. We had to take our own mugs and were given a paper bag containing a currant bun and a fancy (shop made) cake plus lemonade.

A village lady who had a small shop always came with us and we spent our money with her. We also got prizes for any games we won and we could choose what we liked from her basket.

At Easter we went to a field up The Nook belonging to Clarkson's farm where we had egg rolling and various other games. Here, too, the sweet shop lady came and we bought our sweets from her.' *(Barbara Parker – Bolton-le-Sands WI)*

▣ ALL IN THE PAST ▣

'Apart from the usual Church festivals at Lostock Hall – Easter, Christmas etc – the Sunday school Anniversary and the Choir Sermons were eagerly awaited and very much enjoyed by those who took part, and the parishioners who came to the services.

The Sunday school Anniversary was usually held in June. For weeks beforehand the children practised special hymns and on the great day, when they had to attend all three services, those taking part (far more girls than boys) walked up the church aisle singing the processional hymn *We love the place, O God* to a tune written by the Sunday school superintendent, Mr Wilde. All the children sat in the choir stalls or on forms or the chancel steps. The older girls, who had been confirmed, also wore white veils. After the afternoon service everyone had to assemble outside the church institute for a group photograph.

The Choir Sermons was the church choir's special day. They

too would practise special anthems and hymns which they would sing with great gusto at all three Sunday services. Guest ministers were invited to preach and as with the Sunday school Anniversary all the services were very well attended.

Alas, this is all in the past. We at St James' church, Lostock Hall have no Sunday school, hardly any choir and no resident organist. It is sad so few people bother to come to church these days. The church was the centre of village life years ago but sadly not anymore.' *(Pauline Hunt – Lostock Hall WI)*

▣ Our Social Life ▣

'Stopper Lane Sunday school was at Rimington and it began at 1.30 pm so it was a good excuse not to help with the washing up after Sunday lunch.

Sunday school allowed us to enjoy our first taste of independence as we walked the half mile with our friends. There was always lots to do on the way depending on the seasons. We would pick flowers for the table in Sunday school, pick strawberries from the hedgerow, look for birds' nests and in winter make slides on the road regardless of best Sunday shoes.

For the young people of Rimington their social life revolved around Sunday school as public transport was not readily available in the 1950s. We went carol singing at Christmas and had a Jacob's Join tea for the Christmas party followed by good games organised by Uncle Jos, whose wife Mary played the piano. At Christmas we received books as Sunday school prizes for attendance.

Sunday school Anniversary meant two services and it was a good excuse for new sandals for summer and a new dress and cardigan. Best clothes were only worn for Sunday school and special occasions. The highlight of the summer holidays was the Sunday school trip by coach to either Blackpool, Morecambe or Southport for the day. It was very exciting and quite an adventure to go to the seaside.

There was also a Sunday school at Martin Top and we walked another half mile to join in their Anniversary service. The chapel always smelt of apples and flowers when it was the Harvest

Festival, which meant two services. On the Monday night following there was either a slide show (quite a novelty) or a visiting concert party from Clitheroe followed by the sale of fruit and vegetables. It was the main aim of the night to buy a pomegranate and proceed to eat the fleshy red seeds using a pin.

The chapel itself was a plain fronted building closely encompassed with green railings but once inside it was cool, quiet and beautifully kept. There was lovely polished wood and red carpets. The main chapel had a gallery and box pews upstairs and a large two-tier pulpit with ornate ironwork surrounding it with red curtains on the inside. At the back was the Sunday school room with a coal fire and a scullery and a staircase leading up to the magnificent organ and choir stalls, where we sat on special occasions. It was always very exciting negotiating round our Sunday school teacher, who had to pump the organ as we took our seats in the choir stalls to perform our well rehearsed anthems.

This beautiful chapel is no longer a place of worship and has been converted into houses, but the memories still hold firm.'
(Marion Howard – Bolton-by-Bowland WI)

▦ IN THE KITCHEN AT GUNNERTHWAITE ▦

'Gunnerthwaite Farm was owned by my maternal grandparents, and is situated out in the countryside between Arkholme and Borwick.

Every Sunday the "big kitchen" at Gunnerthwaite was transformed when the large dining room table was taken out and replaced by rows of hard wooden forms. Children from all the surrounding area (which was not a village as such but a very large sprawling hamlet) came at 1.15 to Sunday school and at two o'clock parents came for the afternoon service. This tradition began back in the 1800s and continues to this day.

There was a chaise longue at one end under the window with a pedal organ on the right wall. For the Sunday service Grandad and Grandma always sat at the front on the chaise longue facing us, the congregation, and woe betide anyone who fidgeted or was seen whispering. One look from Grandad was enough. At

Children from the Gunnerthwaite Sunday school off on a trip to Heysham Head in 1952. (Emily Hacking – Leck & Cowan Bridge WI)

this time the service was affilliated to the Methodist chapel and local preachers were appointed by the circuit. Arriving by bicycle or on foot, and sometimes by pony and trap having been picked up at the nearest railway station, they always stayed for tea and then went off to preach at the chapel in Arkholme. The farmhouse services have now become independent of the Methodist circuit and appoint their own preachers; the Sunday school is still thriving with 48 children attending at the present date.

The Prizegiving, on Easter Tuesday, was the highlight of the year, when we all dressed up in our Sunday best. Everyone had a recitation to give from memory, and songs and choruses to sing. Following the presentation of the prizes was the supper, after which we all had a romp around. This occasion is still celebrated, but because of the numbers involved the venue has now changed to the nearby Capernwray Evangelical Chapel. I attended there all my life until getting married and moving away, first as a scholar and then as a teacher.

There was always a summer trip, usually to a seaside resort, and Christmas party when parents and friends joined in helping with food and transport. These were great occasions and not to be missed, and are still enjoyed to this present day.' *(Emily Hacking – Leck & Cowan Bridge WI)*

GETTING ABOUT

From horse-drawn traps to steam trains and jet planes, our transport has changed beyond belief over the century.

⚙ WATCHING THE TRAFFIC GO BY ⚙

'I was born in 1906 in the Ormskirk area. We lived just off Liverpool Road, which was known as the Turnpike Road. Half was paved with stone sets for the horse-drawn traffic, and the other half was tarmacked for the bigger motor waggons and traction engines, which carried the huge bales of cotton and other merchandise from the docks to the manufacturing towns in the area.

I used to sit on the garden wall, watching the traffic go by, and I well remember the excitement of a farm fire, and seeing two galloping horses drawing the fire engine to the scene.

By 1919 we were living near Lancaster. The public houses there all had large yards where farmers would leave their horses and traps while they went to the auction. Their wives met up with family and friends, and did their weekly shopping. They often spent all day there, usually on a Saturday.

People without transport thought nothing of walking miles to the nearest towns. Animals were driven on foot, to and from the auction, often several miles from outlying farms.' *(Norah Hargreaves – Overton & District WI)*

⚙ ONE PLACE TO KEEP A HORSE! ⚙

'When I was seven my father changed his job and came to live in

Charabancs were popular for group outings in the 1920s. Hoole chapel choir enjoyed a ride in the open air on their day out. (Betty Gilkes – Hoole WI)

Bolton. We managed to rent a house near the top of Halliwell Road, in a row of ten very nice cottages.

My mother, father and I lived in the second house and in the tenth lived a rag and bone man. He had a pony and cart to collect his wares. His cottage was much smaller than the others and had no back door or garden. He left his cart outside his front window but it was not until I had lived there about a week that I found out he kept his pony in the house.

This fascinated me so much that every day after tea I would go and watch him lead the pony through the front door, through the small front room into the kitchen. We lived there four years and all that time the pony lived in the house. Nobody complained; they all took it for granted.' *(Mona Ridings – Little Lever WI)*

◼ CYCLING DAYS ◼

'In the early 1930s my grandparents were living down White

Dr Duckworth's car was one of the first seen in Eccleston – this picture was taken outside Hawthorn House after an election campaign. (Eccleston WI)

Horse Lane at Barton. On our way to visit them on Sunday afternoons we would pass a large corrugated iron barn just over the hedge. It had been fenced off from the field beyond and several small windows, made in the sides, had clean net curtains.

A buxom lady called Mrs Coppin lived there and made a living of sorts by providing meals for cyclists. The CTC badge was on the wall by the door and at weekends there would be 20 or 30 bikes propped against the fence with one or two riders busy mending punctures while the others enjoyed anything from an enamelled mug of strong tea to a plate of ham and eggs.

If it was very warm they would all help to carry the wooden

A Jowett car in the 1920s, when car ownership was just beginning to spread. (Joyce Simm – Crag Bank WI)

trestle tables outside, followed by long wooden forms or benches, and help serve the food while Mrs Coppin did the cooking or bustled about in her massive wrap-around "pinny" (apron) replenishing tea from the biggest metal tea pot I had ever seen.

Rumour had it that some of her customers would sleep on the floor or the benches on Saturday nights or Bank Holidays, but the only "facilities" were a tin bowl of water on a stool by the door, for washing after repairs. I have no recollection, but there must have been an earth closet somewhere at the back.

We lived by the A6 road and on Sunday evenings there were cycling clubs of 20 or 30 members riding sedately home, two by two, with great bunches of wild flowers, especially bluebells, tied on handlebars or saddlebags.' *(Irene Gregson – Cabus WI)*

❖ TRAINS AND PLANES ❖

'At the age of four in the 1920s, along with my parents and one year old brother, I returned to the house where I was born. It was the grocer's and off-licence from which my maternal grandparents were retiring. This was in Winton, Eccles, close to the historically famous Manchester to Liverpool railway. Nearby was the first Manchester Airport at Barton. A good place from which to view the planes was from the railway embankment. Then we called them "aeras".

We took an interest in the destination of the trains and whether they had stopped at nearby Patricroft station. Amongst the non-stopping trains were two which roared past at 10 am and 10 pm daily, the Irish Mail trains on the way to Holyhead. I was very excited when I travelled on the night train en route for Ireland, aged seven years.

I cannot recall the first plane I saw as they were often seen over our streets. Prospective pilots were learning to fly and five-shilling pleasure flights were available. Going to the airport was a popular Sunday afternoon walk, to view the planes from the perimeter of the tarmac. Ice creams were on sale and the hotel built there is still called the Airport.

I remember clearly the day we saw the first monoplane. Everyone seemed to be looking skywards. As they travelled more slowly than the biplanes we could see them clearly. From then onwards we children were no longer as interested in biplanes and always looked for the monoplanes.' *(Joan White – Little Lever WI)*

◈ NEARLY A FLYING FLEA ◈

'In 1936 there was great excitement where I lived at Wycoller, when seven local men who were inventors "before their time" decided to build an aeroplane on our land. Two of these men were older brothers of my school friend. The plane was to be called the Flying Flea and the land had to be registered as an aerodrome and have a name. The name chosen was BV Aircraft. Many people from around the area came to see the Flying Flea Hut in which the aeroplane was being constructed, but unfortunately, although the large wings and fuselage were built, the Flying Flea never flew owing to trouble with the type of engine used.' *(Margaret Diggins – Trawden & Winehall WI)*

An outing by pony and trap in the 1920s in the Accrington area. (Lucy Day – Barton WI)

◈ LAST TRAIN TO PRESTON ◈

'Sunday, 6th September 1964 was the night the Preston to Southport railway line died. I remember the last train passing through Longton full of revellers singing *Auld Lang Syne*, waving and cheering. The station was full to bursting with people wanting to be part of this historic occasion.

Having lived in Longton for only three years it was still a novelty for the children to be taken across the fields to wave to the trains – steam only. How convenient it was to get the train to Preston for shopping or to Southport for a treat, wheeling the pram into the guard's van for a day trip to the sea.

Within a few weeks of the closure gangs of workmen were lifting the track and dismantling bridges and lineside buildings until all that was left of a once busy line was the fencing either side of the track bed. Thirty years later the stretch is almost unrecognisable. Longton station site is a housing estate, the track bed has been swallowed up by fields and part has been converted into a road to eliminate a dangerous crossroads.' *(Netta Brodrick – Hoole WI)*

HOUSE & HOME

M.Lynskey

THE WAY WE LIVED THEN

*F*rom *two up, two down terraced houses to country cottages, the way we live has changed so much from the days when we made pegged rugs to cover bare floors, used candles to light our way to bed and when layers of warm but restricting clothing were a necessity.*

◈ A LITTLE HOUSE IN BLACKBURN ◈

'I was born in Dublin, Ireland. My father had worked in the shipyards but served in both the British Army and Navy during the Great War and afterwards went into the Merchant Navy (cargo boats). When trade was bad and the civil fighting in Ireland showed no sign of stopping we all came to England for Father to get work here.

At first we lived in Waterloo (near Liverpool) in rented rooms but a friend of my mother from Blackburn came to see us and was horrified to see what we had to put up with – mice and all! It was through her that we got a little house to rent in Lancaster Street in Blackburn and the rent was four shillings a week. The rent man came every Friday night to collect it.

There were only two rooms downstairs and two bedrooms. The lavatory was at the bottom of the yard and between it and the back wall was the ash midden. All our ashes and other rubbish (which my mother always wrapped up well in newspaper) were left there. The dust cart came each week and through a trap door in the wall they shovelled it all out and then Mother cleaned it out before we started again. Happily, because we all hated it, this system was changed soon after we moved in and we all got brand new metal dustbins.

We had a zinc bath which hung on a nail in the wall in the backyard. We lived in the back room in which all the cooking, washing and ironing was done and where we played when we couldn't play outside. We called it the "kitchen".

The blackleaded range was often the heart of the kitchen, as here at Gornalls Farm, Over Wyresdale in the 1930s. (Catherine Tallentire – Abbeystead WI)

The front room was only used on Sundays or if we had visitors calling. Some people called this room the "parlour".

We had gas lighting throughout and I hated having to go to the shop for a new mantle when it got broken because they were so fragile that at the slightest jolt they would disintegrate.

The furniture in the kitchen was a bare (deal) wooden table which extended and which was forever being scrubbed. We had plain wooden chairs with spindles down the back, two wooden stools and Mother's rocking chair.

The space under the stairs was where the coalman tipped two bags of coal in the winter – to keep it dry. He only came fortnightly for which we were truly thankful as everything on the shelves and other things kept there had to be taken out and the place cleaned out after the coal dust had settled. The other corner of the room was taken up with the huge mangle and other washing equipment – the latter being the dolly tub, rubbing board and posser, the boiler stick, a huge scrubbing brush and the gigantic everlasting block of carbolic soap which we had to "peel" for the boiler.

We had white broderie anglaise over-dresses which we wore over our thicker dresses in the winter and cotton print dresses in the summer and they were all starched after washing. It was quite hard to get the creases out when they were dry so we had a bowl of water which we used to flick water over the clothes with our hands. Tablecloths – only used on Sundays and special days – and all the pillowcases were starched. During the week we had a soft oilcloth on the table – like the plastic ones of today and which was easily wiped over. When we were older, just before the Second World War, we got a gas iron and thought how modern we were. It was similar in design to the old box iron but bigger. A flexible tube connected to the gas pipe and you lit it inside and it was just like a blow torch working – and we still had to press down hard. If we thought our ironing was hard, it was a luxury compared to one family who used a newspaper and a hot shovel!

The front room had a large padded wicker armchair and a big polished Windsor chair, a round table with a central support and claw feet and four matching chairs with "plush" seats. There was always a lovely polish smell about them. The sofa had a horsehair seat and was a wretched thing to sit on with bare legs. "Throw-overs" are nothing new, ours came out for the sofa when visitors came! We had a pedestal stand (beloved of photographers) with the traditional blue-bowled aspidistra standing on it. When it rained hard everybody put out their aspidistras in the gutters and that drenching apparently lasted for a long time – I never recall watering or feeding it.

The two bedrooms were very plain except for two lovely small Dutch prints on the wall in Mother's room, which was at the back and was the smallest having only one double bed, washstand and tiny fireplace. Our front bedroom had two double beds – three younger ones in one bed and the two older girls in the other. All the beds had flock mattresses which had to be shaken and pummelled to even them out and we had bolsters which fitted into long cases and tied with tapes. We hated changing them as Mother insisted that "corners were filled" and all tapes had to be ironed flat. The fireplace was only small but much in use if anyone was ill. Mother wasn't keen on using the stone jar hot water bottles after a near disaster with one that leaked.

The beds had "railings" – black with brass knobs on each corner (more polishing!) and both rooms had built-in wardrobes. Mother's travelling chest was at the foot of the young ones' bed and clothes were folded on it every night. We never had the light on in our room just to go to bed as one of the street lamps was directly outside and as we never drew the curtains until we were in bed it saved using the gas. We had to use chamber pots during the nights, having made sure that we all "went" before going to bed and with strict instructions to keep them covered and, of course, use them as little as possible. Our nightly milk or Horlicks was given to us quite early!

When we "graduated" to a coiled spring frame on the beds we thought they were worse to clean. We had a round-headed brush which was put down into every single spring and twirled round – it seemed to take forever! However, the sprung box mattresses were a greatly appreciated boon.

Fashions of the 1920s! (Joyce Simm – Crag Bank WI)

Outside doorsteps and windowsills were stone and after a vigorous scrubbing the downstairs ones – front and back – had to be edged with a donkey stone – a softish stone coloured white or cream. Lintels and door posts were left plain. After doing this the front flagstones had to be swilled clean. If you had any old rags or clothes (highly unlikely!) or enough jam jars they could be exchanged for a donkey stone when the rag and bone man came round with his cart. Although we never saw him with any bones he always called out. "Rags and bones – bottles and jars!"

Windows were cleaned with chamois, dry cloths and polished with newspaper. Upstairs were cleaned outside by raising the sash and sitting on the sill.

When soot began to drop down the chimney that was the time to call in the chimney sweep and although he covered the fireplace with cloths (often sooty themselves) he still made a terrible mess and without a vacuum cleaner then, it was an awful thing to sweep up without it flying round. We liked having to run outside and watch for the round brush head to shoot out of the chimney pot.' *(Jane Burnell – Livesey WI)*

▨ AN OLD FARMHOUSE ▨

'I was brought up in the 1920s in a big old farmhouse with stone floors which were scrubbed every week on our knees. Houses were very bare and cold then. In the kitchen we just had a long scrubbed table and a form behind to sit on. There was no carpet, just a rag rug in front of the old iron range which had an oven on one side and a boiler on the other. The floors upstairs in the bedrooms, and the hall, were covered with linoleum. Chamber pots under the beds had to be emptied and washed every morning, and there were oil lamps to fill and clean every day. We got electricity in 1934.' *(Ethel Stephenson – Over Kellet WI)*

▨ TWO UP, TWO DOWN ▨

'Most of my childhood was spent in a two up, two down terraced house with no garden, but a small flagged backyard in Bury. Getting out of bed on winter mornings needed courage, stepping out on to the linoleum when Jack Frost patterns on the inner surface of the windows bore witness to the temperature. Leaving the cosy warmth of our flock mattresses – huge bags of small felted circles that had to be pummelled back into shape every day – we dressed hurriedly and ran downstairs (again no carpet) to wash at the kitchen sink. Referred to as the "slopstone" this was rectangular, only a couple of inches deep with small brick walls on either side to support it. A curtain on a spring hid the bucket, scrubbing brushes, blocks of household soap and other cleaning aids beneath.

We'd washed with water warmed in a kettle on the gas stove the previous evening, so morning ablutions took place in an enamel bowl full of cold water. Invariably the enamel chipped from these and they leaked. Father would repair them with an arrangement of washers and small screws. Breakfast was eaten at the kitchen table, solid, wooden, square, with four matching lath-backed chairs. Their seats were covered with rexine – a shiny, smooth-surfaced material, cold on even the hottest day.

The front downstairs room had a rexine three-piece suite, sideboard complete with embroidered mat, large wooden clock and brass candlesticks; and a Singer treadle sewing machine given to my mother as an engagement present instead of a ring by my father. It also boasted the only carpet in the house, a square, the stone flags surrounding it painted dark brick-red and polished with special polish.

Our lavatory was situated in a small brick-built addition to the backyard, its inside walls periodically whitewashed with lime by my father. An area in the yard was taken up by the pile of coal necessary for the fires and the yard wall had large hooks on its outer side so that washing lines could be strung across from one row of houses to the other.

All the sash-type windows of the house boasted net curtains on springs covering their lower halves, and longer pairs of fabric curtains pinned on to circular wooden curtain hoops suspended from a wooden rail.

The whole family owned only two books – *The Tolpuddle Martyrs* (courtesy of the Amalgamated Engineering Union, of which my father was a member) and the *Doctor's Book*, acquired by saving coupons issued by a firm selling tea. This latter contained symptoms of various illnesses and I was always enthralled by a photo of an X-ray taken of a child who had swallowed a minute toy bicycle. *(Lillian Zurowskys – Cockey Moor WI)*

▦ A Typical Cottage ▦

'When I was young, before the First World War, my four sisters and I, and mother and father lived in a cottage on the fringe of Lancashire and Yorkshire. It was in a little village called Delph, about three miles from Oldham. It was a typical cottage of the area, with rows of long windows which made the rooms light for the handloom weaving that went on there in the 17th and 18th centuries. Our cottage, which was rented, was built in 1765. Originally, a door opened on to a lane at the back; this was probably used in handloom-weaving days, but was made up before we lived there.

The lavatory was at the bottom of the garden and the night soil cart came round periodically to empty it. In the kitchen was a long stone sink, a "set pot" for boiling the clothes on washing days, a mangle with massive rollers, dolly tubs and a scrubbing board. The "set pot" was enclosed in a brick wall with a space underneath to light the fire for heating the water.

There was an oven and boiler on each side of the fire in the living room. The boiler was filled daily to warm the water for washing up and washing ourselves. A big tin bath was pulled in front of the fire on bath nights (Friday) and we children all used it in turn.

On baking days the fire was pushed under the oven and all the food was cooked in this way. In the centre of the living room was a square table with an oil cloth cover; the table legs were encased in old stockings to keep them from being scratched. On one side of the fire was mother's rocking chair and father's chair was on the other side, and around the room were stand chairs with cushions and also a horsehair sofa.

The sitting room was rarely used, but here was the best furniture – a green plush suite and a walnut sideboard, complete with mirror and shelves. A brass fender surrounded the hearth, together with a brass poker and tongs.

Upstairs, we children had iron bedsteads. We loved them because we could hang upside down on them, turn somersaults or any other ploy that came into our minds. The beds were covered with flock mattresses that had to be turned every day and the flocks spread evenly. They were very heavy and we could never do it satisfactorily for Mother. Once a year the flock beds were emptied on to the floor and the bed tick washed. What a job!' *(Louie Pollard – Gt Harwood & District WI)*

▣ COAL DAYS ▣

'On coal days and dustbin days there was no privacy at our terraced house in Preston in the 1940s. The coalman and dustman entered by the front door and walked straight into the living room.' *(Christina Smith – Ashton WI)*

▣ PEGGED RUGS ▣

'There was always a pegged rug on the go. If there was no knitting, sewing, patching or darning to be done on those long winter nights there was always a rug to be pegged. Every room in the house could boast two or three, usually about three to four by five or six foot, with smaller ones at each doorway. Old discarded coats, dresses, jumpers, cardigans, in fact almost any item of clothing could be used. These were all cut up into small strips about four inches long and an inch wide and kept in separate colours. A well washed hessian sack was the base, a pattern was drawn and then a hole was made into the sacking with a sharp pegging tool, made of wood about four inches long and as thick as your thumb with a sharp point at one end. A peg was then folded in half and pushed tightly into the hole, and so the process continued, putting in the pattern first and then filling in the rest. The rug was then backed with more hessian, and what a weight they were to shake. Every one of them had to be thrown outside and shaken, the most frequently used ones every day, and the rest once a week.' *(Emily Hacking – Leck & Cowan Bridge WI)*

Fashion in 1960 – a needlework class at Manchester day training college. (Lillian Zurowskys – Cockey Moor WI)

▣ A SENSE OF FREEDOM ▣

'As children we were brought up well but led a rather quiet and sheltered life as was the norm at that time. We lived on a farm on the Claughton Hall Estate and attended the local village school.

Everything changed for us in Claughton when a new movement for women was started. All the excitement of this proposal was the talk and topic of that time. Mother joined the Women's Institute as one of the founder members and looked forward to Institute night, cycling to the monthly meetings in all weathers, which had its share of difficulties on some dark nights when travelling on the rough roads – her carbine bicycle lamp would "phut" out – but these and other lesser annoyances wouldn't deter her from reaching the meetings at 7.30 pm.

I remember enjoying some of the results of Mother's cookery classes, given in the winter months by Miss Lillian Sykes, the author of that well known old cook book *The Olio* – my own copy dated 1928.

Then a Glee Club was organised which meant singing practice to be attended and another evening out. Later on, classes were arranged on First Aid given by a member of the St John Ambulance Brigade. Drama classes started too, and all this activity didn't, in some households, go down well with the menfolk, disgruntled no doubt by the fact that they were now left to look after the younger members of the family and see them to bed.

My father, on the other hand, didn't share their opinions, which we were quick to take advantage of when it was time for bed – and he, being the kindest and most indulgent parent ever, would cope with our naughty pranks to stay up later than we were allowed.

My mother was beginning to live a much more fulfilled and satisfying way of life, bringing with it a sense of freedom, something that until then had been denied to country women. *(Gladys Kitching – Claughton-on-Brock WI)*

▣ WHAT WE WORE ▣

'Babies born in the 1920s were kept in long gowns called "barra coats and skips". They were dressed in these for the first six months then "shortened", which meant they were put into dresses – even little boys wore frocks. As they got older the boys wore vests, shirts, trousers which reached below their knees, socks and clogs, a woollen jersey and a flat cap. The girls wore a vest, liberty bodice, combinations, fleecy lined knickers, petticoat, long sleeved frock and a pinafore over the top, plus long black stockings and clogs. We put on our best clothes for Sunday school and church, but took off the "Sunday" clothes when we got home. New-clothes time was always Whitsuntide, when everyone turned out with their families to watch the children "walk" with their churches.' *(Margaret Barrett – Trawden & Winewall WI)*

▣ SOCIAL STRATA ▣

'When social strata were very clearly defined, an explanation for an attractive though penniless middle-aged lady's single state was – "Clogs daren't. Shoes wouldn't!"' *(Jennett Fowler – Ulnes Walton WI)*

WATER AND WASHDAY

*W*hen *every drop of water had to be carried from the well or pumped up into the bucket, washday was a once-a-week drudgery. Few would want to return to those days of no "mod cons".*

▣ NO MOD CONS ▣

'Our house was behind the village shop at Priest Hutton, situated right on the village green. There were no modern conveniences when we first lived there in 1934. There was no water laid on and we did not have a well in the garden like some people, so water had to be carried from a well at the top of the village. To keep local children away from the well, we were told that Jimmy Green Teeth lived in it and he would get us if went too near. Dad used to pay the schoolchildren a halfpenny a bucket to carry water for him in their dinner break from school. They then spent the money in our shop on sweets. My parents were among those who campaigned to have water brought to the village and in 1937 it arrived. A pipeline from Thirlmere to Manchester passed through the parish and we also got our own water supply. The pressure is still very good as it is so near to the main pipe. Electricity came about the same time but a lot of houses did not get that installed until after the Second World War.

We had no bathroom but on Monday it was washday and the fire under the copper was lit in the shed. After the washing was done more water was heated up and we all had a bath. The old zinc bath was brought out into the shed in front of the fire and rested on two pieces of wood. If the wood was forgotten the cold

By 1938, blacksmiths had diversified considerably – this invoice was for replacing an old brown sink with a modern white one after mains water had arrived at Priest Hutton. (June Haythornthwaite – Borwick & Priest Hutton WI)

stone floor could be felt through the bottom. In the winter if it was very cold the bath was brought into the house. After a bath in the shed the water was tipped down the yard and it was brushed with a stiff broom.' *(June Haythornthwaite – Borwick & Priest Hutton WI)*

'We had an outside toilet, which froze in winter and then my father, suitably attired in oil skins, would enter with a blow torch to thaw it out. We had a flush toilet but some people had tipplers which flushed with waste sink water. Baths were, of course, taken in a tin bath in front of the fire. Clean clothes, towels and olive oil to rub on our chests were warmed and always made bathtime a pleasure.

When I was about nine, in 1942, we moved to a house with back and front gardens, a bathroom with a washbasin and inside toilet, and *hot* water. Our relatives thought it was wonderful and so did we.' *(Gladys Gawthorpe – Hapton WI)*

A 'two seater' privy at St Michael's – 'it saved time and was less frightening in the dark with two!' (Judith Hunter – St Michael's WI)

'I grew up in Railway Terrace, Carnforth, in a small house consisting of three rooms up and two down. We were a family of eleven.

Saturday was bathnight. We had a zinc bath and the water was heated in a coal-fired boiler which stood in the corner of the room. Being the youngest member of the family I was always bathed first. I had seven brothers and on one occasion I was in the bath and the boys returned early for tea. My father immediately pushed me and the bath under the table where I stayed getting colder and colder until they had finished their tea and I was then allowed back out to dry in front of the fire.' (*Agnes Newell – Crag Bank WI*)

◧ IT BEGAN ON SUNDAY ◧

'Washing day was Monday but it actually began on Sunday evening when all the clothes were gathered together and sorted into their categories and colours.

On Monday morning all the family were early risers, willing or unwilling, and whilst we were breakfasting Mother lit the fire under the boiler which was alongside the sink, so that when the delicates had been washed they could be rinsed straight away.

The next procedure was a lesson in weightlifting and three-point turns. The mangle was situated under the stairs and this required lifting up a three inch step and then coaxing around a corner and woe betide anyone who touched the paintwork – my mother had muscles like a Sumo wrestler!

My jobs as a youngster, providing I wasn't at school, were to keep the fire going and stir the clothes in the boiler.

Eventually boiled clothes were placed in the dolly tub, which was a large upright tub with a recess for the soap and a rest for the rubbing board, on which I would irritate Mother by being a budding musician. The dolly peg then came into its own – for the uninitiated this is like a cow's udder made out of wood, with four legs and rising in the centre a long pole with cross-handles with which to rotate the clothes first to the left and then to the right; this again required muscle power.

The allocated time for rinsing was decided by Mother who,

dressed in a large pinafore and with a scarf around her head, would then proceed to draw the clothes from the tub and feed them between the mangle rollers. (These were made of wood about five to six inches in diameter.) Then came the ultimate moment of strength, to turn the mangle wheel which drove the rollers. One must remember that the mangle had a cast-iron frame and the wheel was about 14 inches in diameter. There was a large coiled spring on top of the mangle which controlled the tension on the top roller by means of another wheel. Beware anyone who had their fingers caught in the rollers!

When all the clothes had been wrung they were then separated, whites from coloureds. and good old "dolly blue" came into its own. This was a small bag which was put into the water to add to the whiteness. Then followed the starching, which left the pillowcases, tablecloths and napkins so stiff as to cut one's throat and which no self-respecting housewife left out.

The mangle was then manoeuvred back under the stairs, the dolly tub emptied and the boiler fire left to go out.' *(Joan Rackham – Eccleston WI)*

▣ HOLLOW IRONS ▣

'Ironing was a lengthy process. A piece of metal, shaped with a hole at one end, was put in hot coals, then taken out of the fire by means of putting a poker through the hole. It was slotted into the iron, which was hollow for this purpose. Meanwhile another iron shape would be heating up to replace it when the iron cooled down.' *(Winnie Johnson – Goosnargh & Whittingham WI)*

▣ IT GOT EASIER ▣

'It would have been about 1950 when my mother got a washing machine with powered rubber rollers. Washdays were much shorter and much easier after that. When I married in 1959 I didn't have a washing machine to begin with – I had a small boiler and washed by hand. Then Launderettes were opened and my husband used to go into Preston from Freckelton on Friday evenings, while I cleaned the house. The washing came back dry,

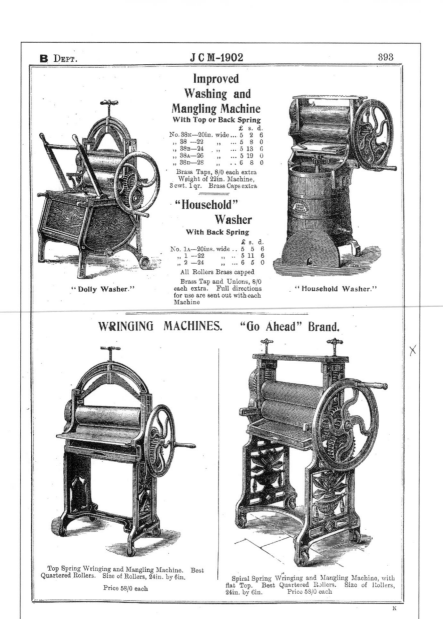

Improved Washing and Mangling Machine

With Top or Back Spring

	£	s.	d.
No. 38ᴋ—20in. wide ...	5	2	6
,, 38 —22 ,, ...	5	8	0
,, 38ʙ—24 ,, ...	5	13	6
,, 38ᴀ—26 ,, ...	5	19	0
,, 38ᴅ—28 ,, ...	6	8	0

Brass Taps, 8/0 each extra
Weight of 22in. Machine,
3 cwt. 1 qr. Brass Caps extra

"Household" Washer

With Back Spring

	£	s.	d.
No. 1ᴀ—20ins. wide ...	5	5	6
,, 1 —22 ,, ..	5	11	6
,, 2 —24 ,, ..	6	5	0

All Rollers Brass capped

Brass Tap and Unions, 8/0
each extra. Full directions
for use are sent out with each
Machine

" Dolly Washer."

" Household Washer."

WRINGING MACHINES. "Go Ahead" Brand.

Top Spring Wringing and Mangling Machine. Best
Quartered Rollers. Size of Rollers, 24in. by 6in.

Price 58/0 each

Spiral Spring Wringing and Mangling Machine, with
flat Top. Best Quartered Rollers. Size of Rollers,
24in. by 6in.   Price 58/0 each

K

*Early washing and 'wringing and mangling' machines – washday was
hard and long! (Jane Burnell – Livesey WI)*

which was wonderful, and he enjoyed his trips because the launderette in Fylde Road had new glossy magazines like *House and Garden* and *Ideal Home*. I didn't have a fridge either, but saved sixpences in a jar and our first fridge cost £32 in 1961.' *(Mary Headley – Caton WI)*

▩ WINTER WASHDAYS ▩

'How I hated winter washdays! Early in the morning the fire under the copper boiler would be lit to boil the water for the "whites". My job was to go to the butcher's for shin beef and trim and cut it up for hotpot before I went to school. The hotpot would cook slowly whilst Mother got on with the washing.

We came home for dinner to find the clothes drying on the maiden around the fire in the living room. Steam was everywhere, condensation on the windows. Back to school and Mother back to the washing. If we were lucky she would be finished when we got home in the afternoon, but then we had the problem of getting it all dry. Still clothes around the fire.

In November we often had drizzling or foggy weather outside and steam and drying clothes inside and we couldn't see the fire. Only as I have got older and we now have washing machines do I realise how tired my mother must have been.' *(Betty Bailey – Astley WI)*

FOOD AND SHOPPING

*F*ood was simpler but home-cooked and often home-produced – the cottager's pig was a mainstay in many households. Tradesmen called at the door every week, and shopping could be a real pleasure.

▩ FLUKES ALIVE! ▩

'Saturday lunch was fish and the fisherman from Flukeburgh would come on the train to Carnforth with his handcart loaded with flukes. As he went along the street he would shout, "Flukes alive, all alive, who'll buy 'em?" My mother would send me with a dish and when he had weighed them he would always add on a small one "for the baby", whether you had a baby or not.' *(Wendy Cowperthwaite – Nether Kellet WI)*

◙ CHEESECAKE PIES ◙
'Before the days of refrigeration it was difficult to keep milk sweet during the summer months. If the milk became suspect it would be heated in a large pan until it became separated and poured through a strainer lined with muslin. The curd was then ready to be made into cheesecake pies simply by sweetening and adding enough beaten egg to make a fairly loose mixture, baked in pastry cases with a few currants on top.' *(Hoole WI)*

◙ FISH AND RABBITS! ◙
'Grandfather went fishing to Glasson Dock at weekends and came back loaded up with cockles, mussels, periwinkles and a few flukes. There was even a rabbit sometimes though I'm not sure he had permission for that! This was dinner for a few days. Other meals included sheep's head for broth – the brains were put in a muslin cloth and cooked in with the lot.' *(Lund WI)*

'Mrs Burrows came round regularly at Overton in the 1930s. She rode a bicycle with a big basket on the front. The basket was lined with a spotless white cloth and was full of shrimps which were sold by the pint or half-pint using two metal tankards. These were not regarded as a delicacy but as part of our normal diet.' *(Myra Sturzaker – Caton WI)*

◙ THE COTTAGER'S PIG ◙
'Pig-keeping in the country districts of Lancashire has been practised way back beyond the span of living memory, and that of most people's predecessors. Pigs, and their products, were the mainstay of a cottager's diet long before fridges and freezers

Clifford Sellers delivering milk at Greenmount post office in 1937 – with Lassie the dog who always followed the trap. (Beatrice Sellers – Greenmount Village WI)

were invented.

A pigsty and an outside washhouse were integral features of the majority of houses built in the latter half of the 19th century in most West Lancashire villages. My grandmother lived in such a house, and in my childhood, I well remember that her walls were decorated, not with useless pictures, but whole flitches of usually fatty bacon, and from her ceiling home-cured hams dangled from hooks screwed into the beams. For protection from the attentions of flies, each item was encased in a double layer of circular-knit cotton stockinet gauze, which allowed for the circulation of air. However, despite such precautions, disasters did occasionally occur, and a constant war was waged upon any bluebottles entering the kitchen, in case a ham or side of bacon should become blown.

As the frequency of public transport improved during the 1920s and 1930s, access to shops became easier for country folk, and the availability of "shop-bought" products minimised to some extent the raising of pigs for home consumption. But when war came in 1939, soon to be followed by food rationing, interest in pig-keeping was rekindled, and those who had suitable premises available "grew their own".

If food was in short supply for humans, it was likewise for animals. All potato peelings were saved, and tiny chat potatoes from farms were eagerly sought after. These, together with kitchen scraps diligently saved in swill buckets, were all boiled up together and made into a mash with meal to form the basis of the pigs' diet. Hideous as this mixture both looked and smelled, it was eaten with obvious enjoyment when served up in the trough.

Well fed and comfortably housed in layers of straw, the pig's life was one of indolence and inactivity. Neighbours and friends would look in at its sty to estimate how many score the cossetted creature would eventually weigh, and at this stage, with its ever increasing girth, a careful watch was kept for any sign of the pig "going off its legs".

Of course, all good things must come to an end, and on the day of execution, the village pig-killer would arrive on his bicycle, equipped with humane killer, and closely attended by his boy apprentice. The event was not without its degree of ceremony. The pig would be led from its sty by two strong men, secured by a rope around its neck. It was an incongruous sight, wearing an upturned bucket upon its head, like a hat, the lowered rim of which acted as a blindfold. The pig-killer's apprentice brought up the rear of this little procession, holding firmly onto the pig's tail in case it should panic and make a bolt for freedom. All this was accompanied by uneasy grunts, rising to squeals of alarm as the victim began to sense that all was not well.

With as many sturdy helpers as it was possible to muster, the difficult bit was to get the unco-operative pig hoisted onto a trestle before it fully realised its impending fate. "Now then, little pig, I'm not going to hurt thee," the pig-killer would croon, with scant regard for the truth. At this stage, pandemonium usually broke out. Terse instructions were bawled above the high-pitched screams of the protesting pig, and the furious barking of neighbouring dogs. Then, with the sharp bang of the humane killer, there was sudden, momentary silence, after which only the dogs continued to bark. Buckets clanked, the pig's throat was cut, and the blood pouring into the buckets was saved as an essential ingredient for the making of black puddings.

Meanwhile, in the washhouse, a fire lighted under the washday copper had heated up a copious supply of scalding water with which the body of the pig was well doused, and its bristles scraped away. Then, well secured with strong ropes, it was hoisted into a perpendicular position against a wall and the full length of the underside slit open, the entrails and all offal being removed. The liver and kidneys were the first meat to be eaten, but the job of butchering proper was delayed for a day or so to allow the carcass to become rigid. A piece of stout wood was inserted into the body cavity to keep the two sides apart.

A plentiful supply of coarse salt was needed to rub into and pack around the two hams and two sides of bacon which were laid upon a stone or concrete bench to cure for several weeks. The salt in those days was supplied compacted in large square blocks, and it was the job of the women of the household to grind these down by slicing at the block in a downward direction with a carving knife.

The rest of the carcass was converted into choice cuts of pork, chops and steak. A "leaf" of fat from each side of the pig was stripped away to be rendered down in roasting tins in the oven. As the fat melted, it was poured off into containers, and set into pure, white lard. The residue of scrams (or scratchings, in modern parlance) were cooled, salted, and eaten with relish, the word cholesterol and its implications not having found its way into the language of the day.

The feet were removed, and served up as trotters to anyone who fancied them, and who had the patience to remove the meat from a multitude of small bones, and lastly, in true semblance of an execution, the pig was beheaded. Once again, the copper was brought into use for the preparation of brawn, it being the only receptacle large enough to accommodate the pig's head. It was not a pretty sight to lift the lid at intervals over the next few hours and see the slowly disintegrating features of what had been, well, almost one of the family!

My grandmother used to say there was a use for every part of a pig, except its grunt, and looking back to those days when the

Preston Pot Fair in 1904, a time to stock up on crockery of all kinds.
(Sheila Main – Garstang WI)

maxim "Waste not, want not" was a much practised virtue, I think she was not far wrong.' *(Evelyn Graham & Margaret Williams – Scarisbrick WI)*

◼ CALLERS TO THE DOOR ◼

'Shopping when I was a little girl in the 1930s was so much easier than it is now. We lived in a village about three miles from the town and yet when my mother went there each Friday it was an effortless exercise; the heaviest purchases she would make would be stamps, haberdashery or occasionally Hawkins' "Little Miss Muffet" printed cotton at 9d per yard for my everyday dresses.

Milk was delivered morning and evening by the local farmer with his horse and float. The milk was measured and poured into the customer's jug and woe betide the unfortunate who spilled milk on the doorstep. Cream came, too, on Sundays. Eggs were freshly laid from our neighbour's hens, with extras "put down" in waterglass in the spring for winter baking. Bread came daily from the village baker, crusty warm loaves delivered on a motorbike with a sidecar. Fresh fish came twice weekly by pony and flat cart (I gather the pony knew its way home when Tommy had had a drop too much – he had a bad chest!).

The butcher had a three-wheeler van, perhaps a forerunner of the Robin Reliant, and he called three times a week, as did another horse and cart bringing fruit and vegetables, but vegetables were mainly grown in our garden.

On Monday afternoon Mr Pike called for the grocery order which was delivered on Wednesday, so on Friday Mother went to town to pay for them and if I was with her I was asked to choose a biscuit from the glass-topped tins which edged the wide polished mahogany counter. The experience was both agony over the choice and bliss with resultant choice. It all seems much more fun and easier than Sainsbury's in the 1990s. *(Pat Hayward – Caton WI)*

▓ AT THE CO-OP ▓

'Shopping was done at the Co-op. The weekly order (about seven items) went in and anything else that was needed was bought during the week. The countermen served you and everything had to be weighed and packed while you waited. Sugar was weighed into blue bags, butter was bought from a tub, and if you wanted treacle, you took your open jar and it was filled by tap from a large container. The main reason for shopping at the Co-op was the "Divi". This varied from store to store and was discussed by friends and relatives for weeks before it was due as plans were made for spending it. New linoleum was always our first priority as by the end of each year it had rotted away on the stone floor and needed replacing. Any spare money was spent on new clothes.' *(Louie Pollard – Great Harwood & District WI)*

▓ SATURDAY TREAT ▓

'As a child in the late 1930s my Saturday morning treat was to travel from Bamber Bridge to Preston, to go shopping with my Grandma. Grandad had a tailor's shop, workroom and house on the main road and my mother, aunt and one uncle worked in the business. Outside the shop on Saturday morning around nine o'clock we waited for the BBMS bus (Bamber Bridge Motor Services) owned by a local family, Prescott's to pick us up. "Hail and Ride" isn't a new venture, most villages then had a small bus operator and Bamber Bridge, pre-war, was little more than the main road and side streets.

We had our regular stalls on the Preston open market (no Market Hall) for fruit and vegetables, then on to Orchard Street for the cheese shop and we could leave our bags from the market whilst we continued shopping. Next we went to Brewers, High-class Grocers, and there was a chair for Grandma and a biscuit for me as we were welcomed by the manager, who knew all his customers by name. Before anything was bought it was a chat about the family or any new product he wished to recommend, then the butter was weighed, patted, marked with the shop crest and wrapped. Sugar, tea, dried fruits etc, were weighed from big boxes and put in various coloured bags with shop labels. The shop had a lovely smell of coffee and spices. Our bags again could be left for collection later.

On, along Friargate, sometimes calling at Bryant's hardware shop, a long passage as I remember, with buckets, brushes, tins hung from floor to ceiling and a little man who had a long stick with a hook on the end to reach for whatever his customer needed.

Into Lune Street and the farmers' wives' stalls outside the Public Hall, so exciting, with puppies and kittens, live chicks and ducks and rabbits for sale. Home-made jams, marmalade, lemon cheese and baskets of eggs and, of course, a lot of chatting.

Across Lune Street to Crooks, a little dark shop down a step (or two) for oatcakes, crumpets, potato cakes. From there to Simpson's Pork Butchers, in Friargate where the Ring Road now is, for home-cured bacon and sausages for the weekend.

Then the shopping bags were collected and off we went to Starchouse Square, another Preston landmark lost to the Ring Road, where other small bus services operated from Viking, Premier and Scout as well as BBMS.

On the way back home, getting on for dinner time, there

The first shop opened by the Rochdale Pioneers – forerunners of the Co-operative Society – in Toad Lane. After the Co-op had moved on, Mr Hopwood took it over. (Vera Walls – Bradshaw & Harwood WI)

would be an extra stop at the driver or conductor's house and his wife would come out with his dinner and tea can, as back in the village they would get a break before their next journey. This was at the terminus, a parking area in the middle of the road where Station Road, Church Road and Wigan Road met by the Hobb Inn, very different today! But Grandma and I got off just before this terminus. The bus would stop opposite our house, the conductor collected our bags, escorted us across the road, put the bags indoors and was rewarded with an apple or orange or a handful of toffees for himself and the driver. Happy days! (*Marie Steinson – Ashton-on-Ribble WI*)

'Every Saturday "going to town" was a must in the 1930s. Hail, rain or shine we trundled off on the tram for a penny, exchanged a paperback book for a penny and came back home with our last penny. In between we walked around every canvas-covered stall, usually with the rain dripping off their edges and down our necks. The market hall and the fish market were covered and it was fascinating to see the Southport ladies in their gingham dresses and floppy poke bonnets selling fresh shrimps. There was even a stall where live poultry were sold. The usual jewellery and materials and the hat market were magnets but it was the cries of the vendors trying to shout louder than anyone else that were really magic.' (*Jane Burnell – Livesey WI*)

FROM THE CRADLE TO THE GRAVE

*W*e were far more likely to be born, to suffer our illnesses and to die in our own homes in the past, though many children faced isolation in hospital when scarlet fever and diphtheria were rife.

▨ HOME CURES ▨

'Country cures included applying baking soda to bee and wasp stings, or rubbing them with a raw onion. There were many remedies for warts – one involved winding a hair from a horse's tail around it and waiting for it to drop off. Others included rubbing the wart with halves of apple or the inside of broad bean pods or leeks.

For cold sores we dabbed the affected part with spirit of camphor every half hour until the stinging subsided. Each family seemed to have had its favourite remedy for sprains. A hot potato poultice applied to the area was one, whilst comfrey in different forms was favoured by many – comfrey oil or an infusion of the leaves applied with a bandage.' (Hoole WI)

'One day when I was little we were going to the greengrocer's, my mother and I, and we passed a group of men retarring the stone sets in the road. There was a large horse and waggon and on the road stood a vat of hot liquid tar. Mother stopped and had a word with the men. Then, to my consternation, she lifted me up in her arms and held me so that my head was over the vat.

"Breathe in, love, it will help to cure your cold," she said. I cannot remember whether I obeyed or not. I was too terrified she would drop me into the cauldron. In those days it was thought the strong smell of creosote or tar would clear the head. She firmly believed she was doing her best for me, but I always see that vat whenever I smell tar.' (May Forrester – Overton & District WI)

◧ THE DOCTOR'S BILL ◧

'In the days before the National Health Service a small charge would be made by the doctor if he made a house call. This was the case when my brother was born, followed exactly twelve months later by my sister. They were both delivered in the front downstairs room.

On another occasion the large front bedroom was prepared as a home operating theatre. The kitchen table was carried upstairs and in turn my sisters and I were laid upon it to have our tonsils removed and my brother was circumcised.' (Sheila Cunliffe – Greenmount Village WI)

Mary Clegg, who died in 1937, was for many years a respected midwife in Radcliffe. Infant mortality was then still quite high and to deliver healthy triplets was considered a rare achievement, which merited a visit from the local photographer. (Eileen Bonnet – Ainsdale WI)

'My father was always ill and the big concern I remember in my youth was the doctor's bill. A man used to call every week to collect money, which amounted to sixpence a week. Mother sometimes was very worried that she wouldn't have enough money to pay but I always remember the man as being very considerate.' *(J. H. – Caton WI)*

▣ SALT AND SOOT ▣

'We never had regular dental checks unless they sent us from school to the clinic (I don't think many people did in the 1930s). We didn't have toothbrushes – we cleaned our teeth with a mixture of salt and soot and it certainly kept them clean and we never suffered any ill effects from it.' *(Jane Burnell – Livesey WI)*

▣ TO THE ISOLATION HOSPITAL ▣

'When I was ten years old I contracted scarlet fever, a most infectious disease, and I had to be admitted to the fever hospital at Luneside, Lancaster. The transport was a horse-drawn ambulance (this was in 1920), and I vividly remember hearing the clip-clop of the horse's hooves as they came nearer. My greatest fear at the time was that it might be "play time" at the school opposite and all the children would see me being carried into the ambulance. I was in hospital for eight weeks and the only contact I could have with my parents was conversation through the window. While I was in hospital my bedroom at home was sealed and fumigated.' *(Margaret Bates – Crag Bank WI)*

'I remember being carried from by home, by nurses in red cloaks, and being taken to the isolation hospital in Longsands Lane, Fulwood because I had scarlet fever. I was there for six weeks and my parents and brother could only try to speak to me from outside the closed windows – which being February was rather cold for them.

Whilst I was away from home the books and toys from my bedroom had to be destroyed, although as it was 1943 there weren't too many of these, and the room had to be fumigated.

Each day I was in hospital my three year old brother used to send me a drawing and it was usually a picture of a local character, our milkman – Mr Lewis – delivering with his horse and milk float. He always wore a spotless white overall and a bowler hat and on the 1st May each year he used to dress up his horse; its mane and tail were plaited and it was decked with ribbons and brass bells.

On my return from the fever hospital I was given, I think by a trust connected to the Great Ormond Street Children's Hospital, a lovely copy of J. M. Barrie's *Peter Pan and Wendy* which I still treasure.' *(Jean Smallwood – Hoole WI)*

◈ VISITED ONCE A MONTH ◈

'In 1937 at the age of six I was taken into hospital. I had been born with a deformed hip and pelvis and after various treatments had been tried and failed it was decided to fix it once and for all. This they did!

I was taken from my mother and grandmother at the hospital entrance, and taken down miles of corridors to the ward. This had only three walls, the fourth was a railing halfway up to the ceiling with an uncarpeted, unlinoed floor and no heating. It was a TB ward. I didn't have it but they thought I did.

My hair was cut *very* short and I was strapped to a frame – my legs spread and strapped separately into a "cap" at the top. Totally immobilised except for my arms, I was put into bed to stare at the ceiling for months. I could hear some awful growls and moans (some of the children were mentally disabled) and I was terrified.

The daily routine was dull. We wakened at 4.30 am to porridge cut out of a bowl in slices, then we were washed. Here I was lucky as I was in the second bed. The bowl of water and cloth was used for all 20 children, similarly the comb was dipped in a bowl of water and again used for everybody. We were never bathed or had our teeth cleaned. We were left until dinner with nothing to do but lie. Dinner was grey, watery mince and potatoes followed by rice pudding, again served in slices. Tea was bread and butter, supper watery cocoa at 5.30 pm. The ward

Funeral cards would be sent to relatives and friends when there was a death in the family. (Emily Hacking – Leck & Cowan Bridge WI)

was locked at 6 pm and we saw no one until 4.30 am next day.

In autumn leaves lay on the beds, in winter snow and mostly rain. To protect us from the rain thick brown leathery covers were attached to the four corners of the bed. This made grooves and hollows which filled into little puddles. If you moved the water came into your bed. You were then clouted and told "serve you right".

Parents visited once a month and we were threatened in case we said a word. Consequently little was said on our part during the three-quarter hour visit. After the parents left, sweets, presents etc were taken from us. At one spell I was in plaster and I shoved some chocolate down the plaster. It melted and stayed there until it was removed for another plaster months later.

The "frame" didn't work and one leg obstinately remained shorter than the other so they decided to stretch it. Thick brownish papers were put into hot water where they became like fly papers and four of these were slapped on to my legs. They had tabs attached at the bottom, weights were added and dangled over the end of the bed, and the bed raised 12 to 18 inches. Every three days the papers were changed. I had hairy legs and yes, they just tore them off. Woe betide you if you cried! This, too, went on for months.

The food and routine never varied except for Christmas Day, when we had chicken, and jam on our bread for tea. I was eventually discharged in plaster into a spinal carriage and left.

Six years ago I was given a replacement hip and had "reconstruction work" done (don't ask!). I received nothing but kindness and endless, patient care and attention.

Good old days? No thanks!' *(Maureen Jackson – Cronton WI)*

CHILDHOOD & SCHOOLDAYS

CHILDHOOD DAYS

*I*t was a different world when we were young. Here are memories
of the freedom we had to play and to grow, and of great affection
across the generations.

◼ BORN IN 1908 ◼

'At Pilling the Angelus bell rang at 7 am, noon and 7 pm each
day from St William's church. Our dog sat in the middle of the
road and "sang" till it finished.

The school trip was to Calder Vale. When we got to the hill at
Barnacre the charabanc stalled and all the children had to walk to
the top of the hill to reduce the load.

Each spring we were dosed with a mixture of brimstone and
treacle to clear the blood from boils and acne. Bitter aloes was put
on nails to stop us biting them. Grandfather always kept a supply
of tincture of quinine, laudanum and iodine in bottles with glass
stoppers on his mantlepiece. Many times he eased our toothache
with a drop of laudanum on a cotton wool swab. Cinder tea was a
cure for babies' wind; a red-hot coal was dropped into a cup of
water and spoonfuls of the liquid fed to the baby.

Cowrie shells and an abacus on casters were used for counting
in school, and button holes were stitched with red cotton on
white cloth. We all wore clogs with irons which made sparks
when struck onto stone or concrete. If we did not wear an oak
leaf on Royal Oak Day the bigger boys chased us and stung us
with a nettle. On Empire Day we marched round the teacher's
lawn carrying flags of all nations, singing patriotic songs.

We bought moleskins, which he had cured, from the local mole
catcher for sixpence and made them into purses with a button
fastener. We made beads from strips of wallpaper and flour
paste, which were wound round a steel knitting needle, and
stuck down. When dry they were varnished and threaded onto
cord or string.

'My grandmother had eight stepchildren and four children from her own marriage. Their house (Springfield Hall in Wigan) had 14 bedrooms. My mother's childhood before the First World War was full of long sunny afternoons as shown here. She is sitting on grandma's knee in the grounds of the Hall, whilst her brothers and sisters shoot and fish.' (Sheila Buchan – Appley Bridge WI)

Grandfather told us stories of shipwrecks on Pilling sands, of men being drowned out fishing and shooting, and a horse and a cart being sucked in by the treacherous quicksands. He made us snow pancakes from the pure white snow we brought in on shovels, which was put into a huge bowl to melt, then mixed with flour. He fried in butter the snigs (eels) he had caught in the brook, and played tunes from the lovely violins he made. Then we sang and clapped the following rhyme:

There was a man, a man indeed who sowed his garden full of seed
When the seed began to grow 'twas like a garden full of snow
When the snow began to melt 'twas like a ship without a belt
When the ship began to sail 'twas like a bird without a tail
When the bird began to fly 'twas like a diamond in the sky
When the sky began to roar 'twas like a lion at my door
When the door began to crack 'twas like a stick across my back
When my back began to bleed 'twas time for me die indeed.'
(Helen Lawrenson – Calder Vale WI)

❖ MY GRANDFATHER ❖

'Every time I see the yellow coltsfoot opening its bright eye I think of my grandfather and long days ago when I was a child.

He was the nicest man I have ever known, with his bright blue eyes and white moustache. Grandma would take him to task when he sat me on his knee and promised to buy me a doll's pram or a bicycle, but I knew it was just pretend and that he would have, if he had the money. His trade was a carpenter, and instead he made me a little rocking chair and a doll's cradle on rockers, which to me was far better.

He loved the spring flowers and I would rush round to him with a bunch of coltsfoot which he would take with great joy. "The first flowers of spring," he would say and put them in an eggcup and stand them on the windowsill. Later it would be bluebells, then buttercups, which had pride of place in a jam jar. I also remember taking him little bunches of grass when I could find nothing else. These he treated with care and put in water also!

My grandfather didn't retire until he was 80 years and first started to do half-time when he was eight. Sometimes in the summer days I would go round to my grandma's and wait until he came home from work. My grandma would put the cloth on the table and set it ready for tea. I would hide beneath the table

'My earliest childhood memories are of Grandad, Ben Alty, and his old thatched cottage at Pilling. There was always a pot with glue warming on the hob which Grandad used when making violins. He also gave violin lessons and painted pictures, including this self portrait. As children we often visited, walking over the fields from Stakepool. We loved to go as there was always something new to do and see.' (Edith Robinson – Cabus WI)

and make whistling noises. "Is there a little bird in here?" he would say when he came in, pretending not to know I was there.

Alas, as I grew older I neglected to go round as often as I should, my mind filled with other things, until my grandma died when I was twelve. Then my grandfather was very sad and I tried to comfort him. They had been married for more than 60 years, having celebrated their Diamond Wedding anniversary, and she had borne him twelve children. My heart fills with tears now as I remember him, with his head in his hands and the grandfather clock standing in the corner ticking the time away.

However, he rallied round and I became his constant companion. On school holidays I would call round to cook his breakfast. He loved fried tomatoes and would send me to the market to buy the deep red, sweet kind and I remember that they cost 4d a pound. These he would have with bacon, eggs and fried bread. I cooked this feast in a big frying pan on a gas ring in the stone-flagged kitchen of his little house.

Sometimes if he wasn't feeling too well I would shave him, under his instructions. Other times we would go for walks, to visit the woodyard where he had worked, and he would tell me of places he remembered long ago that were once all fields and where he used to walk when he was a young man.

He died on the eve of his 89th birthday, after a short illness, on the bed he had shared with my grandma, watched over until the early hours by his loved ones. His birthday cards lay on the mat unopened.

They wrote about him in the local newspaper, a tribute to a grand old man who had helped pioneer the first trade union in the town (Rochdale) but I didn't know about that. I remembered him for his kindliness and his patience, a memory that still remains after more than 60 years.' (*Vera Walls – Bradshaw & Harwood WI*)

▣ Bridging the Centuries ▣
'Those of us who were fortunate enough to be born in the 1920s, between the two wars, have a real perspective of both the 19th and the 20th centuries. We had Victorian grandmothers who by their memories and attitudes could transport us back into the

early 19th century, and possibly by the stories they had passed down to them, into the 18th century! Our mothers in the Twenties were "flappers" with recently bobbed hair, short skirts and Charleston tendencies. They looked forward with confidence to the brave new world where women would no longer be chained to the kitchen sink. They were liberated women who queried the old values and customs of their upbringing. "Don't be old fashioned!" they said to our grandmothers, who viewed some of their ideas with horror.

My earliest memories are always of my Grandma's. I regarded it as the nearest thing to heaven. Everything was always put back into its place, and things happened in sequence.

I slept with my Grandma in a wonderful high feather bed. The bedroom had rose patterned wallpaper, and when I was alone in the summer months I counted the roses. I always fell asleep before I'd finished. In winter I went to bed with Grandma. I knelt with her as she said her prayers, and thought how long she took, it seemed an eternity.

On Saturday nights I sat by the fire and she told me stories of Christmas long ago; when each child had a sixpence in the toe of his or her stocking, an orange, a few sweets and a little wooden toy or doll; of schooldays in Pilling when she paid 5d each week for her schooling; of turf cutting and potato getting; and the great yearly trek to Blackpool, which was really a kind of glorified picnic. After the Shard Bridge was built in 1862, children from Over Wyre joined together from the village and walked to Blackpool. There was, of course, safety in numbers. They took food and a drink and as many pennies as they had saved. It must have been a wonderful day out, and my Grandma had in her cabinet little souvenirs, all marked "A present from Blackpool". The older children looked after the smaller ones in their own families, and after a paddle and a donkey ride, they set off home again.

My maternal Grandma was given a miniature wheelbarrow for her seventh birthday. This was to help cart the turves to the edge of the field where the delving was taking place. Some of the turf would be for their own fires, and rest to be sold in the newly developed towns of Fleetwood and Blackpool.

I lived in two worlds. The first a world of flush toilets, and what

I thought of as "snobby" children. They called my clogs "clunter clogs" and openly criticised anyone who stood out through lack of "good" clothes or toys. My second world was Over Wyre, where different games were played, toilets were little houses with boards with holes in them and buckets underneath, and even schools had these. One I attended had a board scrubbed daily with five holes in it! Unfortunately, the doors for removing the buckets were in the boy's playground which led to many "incidents" where innocent young girls were "upset" by spies!

There were also boggarts! Every road in the Over Wyre area had one on its lonely lengths. Sometimes two! There was the Carr Lane Cat, the horse boggart of Hackinsall Hall, the spotted dog boggart in Pilling, the Burnt House Lane boggart, and the Green Lane boggart. One I knew all about because I heard it! Oh, yes I did. I was six years old and I have never forgotten the experience. My father had put me on a bus in the care of two young ladies who were returning from work. My uncle met me off the bus, and gave me a ride on the back step of his bicycle. I clambered on and we set off. The carbine lamp made a spurting noise. I chattered, and talked still more as I alighted when the road became steeper. Suddenly there was a tremendously loud crunching noise on my side of the bicycle. I jumped in fear and clung to the bicycle frame, causing a full stop. "Hold your noise, and leave go," said my uncle in a gruff and unusual manner. The noise continued, and by now I was really afraid, but I wasn't going to show it to this nasty bad-tempered uncle who was usually so benign. The noise followed us up the hedgerow and we continued up the road until we came to a gate in the hedge. Here the noise stopped. My uncle and I continued up the hill to the house, one on each side of the bicycle, and both utterly silent. He strode up to the door and flung it open. "We've heard the Boggart," he announced.' *(Mary Parkinson – Stalmine with Staynall WI)*

◪ CHILDHOOD ON THE FARM ◪

'Childhood days on a farm beside the river Hodder in the 1920s were idyllic. Calves, lambs, chickens, kittens, sometimes a foal – all these young animals were our playmates.

Children watching the sheep washing in the Hodder river. (Agnes Walker – Broughton WI)

We had our share of jobs to do after school or during school holidays. One highlight the youngsters of today can never experience was the day my father washed the sheep. This had to be done to clean the wool before clipping and what better place than the deep pool in the river under the "old bridge". Sheep, horse-cart and hurdles were taken down to the "bathroom" on the shingle. There was always a gathering of children, our own or neighbours', whether to help or just watch I'm not sure. There was much baaing and bleating and much struggling as the sheep were well and truly "dunked".' *(Agnes Walker – Broughton WI)*

▣ AT NETHER KELLET ▣

'My first recollection of Nether Kellet where I was born is of a small peaceful village nestled amongst the hills.

The centre of the village was built around a piece of common land that had been open until the Enclosure Act, when it was walled in. There were many more trees about the village than there are today and quiet lanes, beautiful woods to walk in amongst carpets of bluebells in abundance, primroses, wood anemones, lily of the valley and many more different species of wild flowers. Wild strawberries and hazel nuts were there for the picking but alas no more because of the large-scale quarrying we have today. The main occupation at that time was farm work, lime burning and quarrying in a small way.

I was born in the same house my mother was born in, 4 Jubilee Cottages. My grandmother had died and Mum continued to live there even after she married so as to look after my grandfather. I have wonderful childhood memories of living there. Our home was next to one of the village water supplies which came from underground springs. The water was cold and crystal clear even on the hottest day in summer and it never dried up.

The workmen came round in the summer to tar the roads and cover them with chippings. Along would come Mr Hodgeson with his big steam roller to go up and down over the chippings. When it was a very hot day the tar bubbles would appear and this was a child's delight to sit and burst them! My mother often found me doing just that. Off she would take me into the kitchen and rub my hands with butter to get it off. What a task that was.

One could play on the roads in those days, they were so quiet. We hardly saw a car and the bus from Lancaster was only twice a week on Tuesdays and Saturdays. We had a lot of fun playing hopscotch, whip and top, marbles, ball games, tig, tin-can-purky. We had lovely rhymes for when the skipping ropes were brought out and we had all the actions to go with the rhymes. Also, during the summer, we played with shuttles and bats.

Sometimes we would go to the tip to look for pottery, old pans, a kettle, anything we thought we could use to make a little house in the plantation at the top end of the village. How we used to love haytime when we could ride in the empty carts that would be going back from the barns to the field. It was just as exciting when the thresher visited the farms and we could watch all the activity that went on at that time. Then there would be the fun of making tunnels with the bales of straw in the barn. If we were found out we would be in great trouble. We were never bored in those days; we had lots of fun and found plenty to do. Childhood for me was a wonderful, happy time.' (*Florence Holden – Nether Kellet WI*)

▣ MEMORIES OF THE CO-OP ▣

'The Co-operative Movement embraced all our family: my father was a member of the Men's Debating Class, my mother a member of the Co-operative Women's Guild, and I attended a class for juniors led by a Mr Kimberley. My elder sister, ten years older than me, worked in the Co-op bakery which was above the Co-op stores in Albert Road, Colne.

The best part of the Co-op as far as I was concerned as a child was the Fellowship meeting on Saturday evening. Some weeks it would be for adults only if it was a lecture not considered suitable for children, but most Saturday evenings my mother, father, myself and two younger brothers would be there at Shackleton Hall, which was a very large room with a stage and a maple wood dance floor. We would queue along with many other families, ascending from Church Street up a narrow flight of stairs, and after leaving our coats in the cloakroom we would enter the hall which would be filled with rows of chairs facing the stage. Children were encouraged to sit at the front of the hall and this we did. We were often entertained by a concert party consisting of a pianist, male and female singers and occasionally a ventriloquist or a magician, which we children liked best of all.

At "half time", as we called it, we had cups of tea and a bun. The tea was served from large teapots with or without sugar and the buns or cakes came from the Co-op bakery. After the supper interval the chairs were moved back around the walls of the room and dancing commenced.

I loved dancing from an early age and aged nine or ten I would be most disappointed if I didn't get to take part in the Lancers, a fairly complicated partner-swopping dance which I was very proud to have mastered.

The Co-op Fellowship held rambles in summer to Kelbrook, Earby, Barrowford – always on the day of Barrowford Show – and also a ramble by train to Skipton.

As I grew older I found other hobbies and interests but I have never forgotten the happy times I had with all the other Co-op members and their families.' (*Vera Clarke – Trawden & Winewall WI*)

◪ HELPING GRANDMA AT BLACKPOOL ◪

'My Grandma was a Blackpool landlady and on Saturdays during the season, through the summer and up to the end of the "lights", my brother Sydney and I used to help her get ready for the next week's visitors.

Dad would drop us off on Saturday morning and go on to his job as manager of Coop & Naylors, stationers and bookshop on Abingdon Street. The last week's visitors would be going home and the children would be running about getting their buckets and spades, and swimsuits off the line in the backyard, wanting one last look at the donkeys going down the street on to the promenade. Mums and Dads would be packing their cases ready for the walk to Talbot Road bus station which was just at the bottom of the street, or for those that lived further afield to Blackpool North railway station to go on to Tyneside or Scotland.

The crowning of the Rose Queen at Trawden – many of us took part in such ceremonies during our childhood. (Margaret Barrett – Trawden & Winewall WI)

Visitors used to book for the next year in advance, usually the same weeks each year, but sometimes there would be vacancies so the cards had to go up on the sash windows: "B & B, Vacancies, Full Board, Apartments." The mother of the family bought all the main food, for instance bacon and eggs for breakfast, while Grandma provided cereal and milk, bread, or toast if wanted, and pots of tea, and in the evening the mother provided the main course meat or fish and vegetables. Grandma provided the potatoes. This, of course, was an excellent way of mother paying only for what her family would eat, and father could have steak whilst she and the children had sausages. It could, however, be quite confusing in the kitchen because you had to make sure you didn't get everyone's food mixed up. Each family had their own little cupboard or "meat safe" in the dining room to store their food in and they used to pay a few coppers for use of "the cruet".

When the visitors were on their way home we had to get ready for the next lot, clean out the dining room and empty the cupboards – nearly every family left half a bottle of ketchup or HP Sauce and the next visitors brought a new one, I don't think Grandma ever bought any. Also, if we were very lucky they would leave all their empty pop bottles and Sydney and I would collect them up in a wicker basket and take them back to the off licence where we would get the deposit back, quite a nice little treat, and buy ice cream or pop ourselves. This treat came later in the afternoon however, because all the rooms had to be cleaned and the beds changed. I was in charge of stripping the beds and Grandma remade them after we had struggled between us to turn the mattresses. There were no en suite facilities then and Grandma was in charge of collecting the chamber pots which were made available for those who got "took short" in the night.

Once the beds were stripped the washing had to be done. Grandma had a big boiler in the washhouse and as the sheets were washed and then rinsed she passed them to Sydney and I, out in the yard. I guided them through the rollers and he would turn the handle of the mangle; this was a job where we both needed wellingtons and sometimes we would fall about laughing and drop the sheet back in the drained water and have to do it all again. The sheets were heavy linen, no polycotton then, and Grandma would hang them up using wooden dolly pegs on rope lines all across the yard. The sheets could give you a nasty whack if the wind got behind them.

In the school summer holidays I sometimes used to stop all week and my brothers would stop at home with Mum. I would sleep on a camp bed in Grandma and Grandpa's living room and they would be on the studio couch having given up their bedroom for the visitors. We would do all the usual jobs and I would help serve breakfast and do the washing up. Then we would go to St John's or Abingdon street market to do the shopping. The stallholders in St John's market all knew my Grandma and my mum and her sister Norma as they had grown up in George Street, and grandma would proudly show me off as "our Joyce's girl" and they would tell me how like my mum I was. We sometimes went to the UCP tripe shop in Cookson Street, Grandad was a great one for trotters and tripe. Tripe was all right in white onion sauce with mashed potatoes but he used to have the trotters in a pint bowl of boiling water smothered in vinegar. I can hear him enjoying them to this day.

Helping Grandma came to an end in 1959 when Dad got a job in Preston. We moved to Brindle Road in Bamber Bridge to adventures new, riding the country lanes on our bikes, paddling in chuckling fells and picking blackberries, and Grandma bought a twin tub and gradually changed her rooms into self-catering flatlets.' *(Carol Smith – Clayton-le-Woods WI)*

▣ GROWING UP ▣

'In the 1920s the Sunday afternoon meeting place for boys and girls in Bolton-le-Sands was the "monkey rack" wall at Whin Grove. The village bobby patrolled and a smack with his large leather gloves controlled any infringement of good behaviour.

Parents were strict and sex was a word unknown. It was a terrible disgrace to be unmarried and "in the family way". We all knew we would be thrown out of the house if this happened. Fear was the greatest deterrent. Mothers never discussed any intimate details of sex and marriage. We had never seen a man's naked body until marriage. There was no permissive society in our young days.' *(Margaret Sanderson, Marian Rigg – Bolton-le - Sands WI)*

'Mother joined the Women's Institute in 1922 and when I was 14 I was allowed to go with her to meetings and promised when I was 15 I could become a member.

Unfortunately the day I was to join was the day I had to help out at an aunt's farm. I started at 8 am and worked until 7 pm and was almost afraid to ask if I could finish early.

My day included making butter in a big end-over-end churn, drawing endless buckets of water from the well (there was no tap water at all), bringing in peat from the farmyard, and scrubbing stone floors and polishing the doors with beeswax. They needed a lot of rubbing to get a shine. The big fire grate had a large well underneath and the ashes were emptied once a week. As only peat was burned the ashes were like fine white powder and very dusty. Water was poured into the well and mixed to a paste with a long-handled spade, ladled out into a barrow and wheeled out to the farmyard.

I was given half a crown for my day's work and I remember thinking – if I pay two shillings for my membership I shall have sixpence change and with threepence more I can still go to the dancing class, which was ninepence, at the end of the week.' *(Edith Robinson – Cabus WI)*

❖ SPARKING CLOGS ❖

'In 1942 my family moved from Tyneside to Rossendale. At that time my brother was at junior school, and his chief ambition was to own a pair of clogs like many of the children in his class. He envied them their ability to make sparks with clog-irons on the pavement. Eventually my mother bowed to pressure and reluctantly bought him some. From that time he wore them almost every day. Our neighbour was heard to say: "When that there lad runs down't back lane sparkin' 'is irons on't pavement, it fair shakes our chandelier!"' *(Monica Chesworth – Over Kellet WI)*

❖ RINGLETS ❖

'Until I was eleven I had long waist-length hair, which had to be combed and plaited every day, except on very special days when it was put into ringlets.

One such occasion was when I was to be bridesmaid for my Aunty May, when I was about five years old in 1947. Out came the "rags", which were strips of cotton material about two foot six inches long and an inch wide. One end was held over the head at nose level and wet tresses of hair were wound around the other end from the nape of the neck. This was repeated 20 or so times until all the hair was bound, then the loose end was wound over the bound tress and knotted at the bottom. Of course, as the hair dried it pulled tighter and tighter, usually

Those ringlets – little Emily on her best behaviour in 1947. (Emily Hacking – Leck & Cowan Bridge WI)

overnight – ouch! But it was well worth it when the rags were removed and all those lovely ringlets bounced around your head, with ribbons tied at the temples to complete the hairdo.'
(Emily Hacking – Leck & Cowan Bridge WI)

GAMES AND TREATS

Games had their seasons and we all seemed to known when it was time to put one aside and take up another, usually using the roads as our playgrounds.

❖ TREATS AND SWEETS ❖

'Father Christmas brought us new clothes, vests, knickers, socks and liberty bodices, but we always got one toy each. During the depression in the 1930s when Father was out of work the church at Bradford ran a community centre for the men at which they were taught, amongst other things, how to make toys – so we also had one big toy to share, such as a dolls' house complete in every furnishing detail, a blackboard and easel, bagatelle and board skittles as well as board games and jigsaw puzzles – all home-made.

Exchanging "scraps" was a favourite game. These were coloured pictures of flowers, fairies, cherubs, angels, clowns and nursery rhyme characters. One big one was worth two small ones and we usually sat with our friends on the doorstep to do the "swapping".

Outside, "shops" were played on the big flat stone by the factory gate. We fashioned all kinds of wonderful things from the clay and used broken pottery for money – any with gold on it was very valuable. As the mill workers took their own pots and "brew" to work there was always *some* broken china there. Other games outdoors were "piggy", a ball catching game; rounders; french cricket; and catching against a wall with one or two balls; and also bouncing rhymes.

Leyland Methodist church's Brownie pack in 1933. (Monica Chesworth – Over Kellet WI)

Games came in seasons. There was whip and top for a while, then marbles, followed by skipping (with straw ropes knotted together which the father of one of our friends got for us from the wholesale fruiterers where he worked). We also made a long loop from them and threw it over the arm of the lamp post where it rested in a groove, then we folded our coats over it for a seat and swung round the lamp post. We played team skipping games where two people held a long rope and we skipped in and out until someone was caught by the leg (usually on purpose!). For skipping on our own we were delighted to get some proper ropes later, either for Christmas or a birthday.

We had singing games – "Farmer wants a wife" and other action songs like British Bulldogs and Roman Soldiers.

Playing out in the street was comparatively safe as there was very little traffic other than the horses and carts. In fact we all ran out to watch any motorcar that came down! We "paddled" in the summer. Mother put her bedding in the zinc bath (known as a "bungalow" bath) and we all pounded it with our feet. We played in the snow and loved to make big "pads" of snow on our clogs, always trying to make ours higher than anyone else's.

All outdoor games were forbidden on Sundays, mainly because of the noise we made! Indoor ones were allowed but we had lots of books – prizes from Sunday school – and we were encouraged to read them to each other, which was often a source of great hilarity, but we all really liked it best when our mother read to us.

On rare occasions we went to "the pictures". Known officially as "The King's Hall" it was locally christened by all its patrons as "The Scrat", although we never had any trouble with livestock! There was only carpet on the floor in the tuppennies which they took up for the Saturday afternoon matinees. We didn't mind the bare floor in the penny section; we could bang on it with great vigour when the "goodies" were overcoming the "baddies". Although they still showed some old silent films with captions, we saw lots of Laurel and Hardy and occasionally the "big" film being shown for the evening. Cowboys and Indians were the usual films and there was also a twelve episode serial as well as the Pathe newsreels, when all the boys crowed with the cock at the start and got a sharp tap from the man with the long pole which he used to open and close the shutters.

When we got a half-penny to buy sweets we bought "Spanish sticks", liquorice, which we sometimes put in a bottle (chopped up) and filled it with water, giving it several shakes during the day. After about three days under the stairs it acquired a lovely sludgy colour and our "Spanish juice" was ready to drink. It was topped up several times until it disintegrated and Mother made us throw it out.

We never got regular spending money so sweets were a rare treat, especially if our parents' friends (honorary aunties and uncles) bought sweets or small bars of chocolate on our birthdays or at Christmas.' *(Jane Burnell – Livesey WI)*

▧ PLAYING IN THE ROAD ▧

'There were very few cars on the roads in those days (the 1940s) and I can still see all us children in the neighbourhood playing

'This photograph was taken on what is now the A682 in Blacko in the early 1930s. What bliss it must have been for Audrey to pedal about in peace and safety. Now one takes one's life in one's hands attempting to cross the road.' (Jean Brown – Blacko WI)

hopscotch, spinning tops with a whip (a stick with string at the end) and skipping with the clothes line stretched across the road. We did have to move for the occasional car, and for the horses and carts – and the job we most hated was collecting the horse muck off the road for use on the allotment!' *(Joan Ditchfield – Moss Side WI)*

SCHOOLDAYS – THE BEST YEARS OF OUR LIVES?

Generations of children have memories of long walks to school, coal fires in the classroom, strict discipline and times tables!

▣ GETTING THERE ▣

'My schooldays started at the age of five in 1920. Being a farmer's daughter I lived about a mile and a half from the village school at Newton in Bowland. Some children were three miles away at least – making six miles to walk by the time they reached home again. The ones with the longest distances to come usually started school when they were six years old.

Our footwear was clogs – wooden soles with clog irons on. They kept one's feet dry! A few scholars in the summertime wore plimsoles which were a new fashion. They were made from a soft dark canvas and had rubber soles. What a change when you couldn't hear your own footsteps. But I remember on the rough paths you knew when you'd stepped on a stone!

If you lived in the village you went home for dinner but we who didn't carried our sandwiches and cakes in our dinner baskets. In winter a large kettle was put to boil on the big round iron stove to provide us with a hot drink.

Occasionally if the wind was in the wrong direction the fire wouldn't burn up so we had to do without our hot drinks. In summer time we drank from the well which was across the road from the school.' *(Edith Lawson – Slaidburn WI)*

HINDLEY AND ABRAM GRAMMAR SCHOOL.

Report on Term ending *July 26th* 19 19

	MAXIMUM 100.
Name *John Greenhalgh*

Age on August 1, 19 *18* Y *11* M *9*

Form *III a.* Average Age Y *12* M *1*

Number in Class *28*

Scripture	... ...	41
Writing	... ...	55
Dictation	... ...	60
Composition	... ...	60
Grammar	... ...	75
Literature	... ...	45
History	... ...	63
Geography	...	64
French		44
Latin	... ...	
Arithmetic	... ...	50
Algebra	... ...	89
Geometry { Pure / Appl.		70
Trigonometry	...	
Mechanics	...	
Physics { Theory / Practical		52
Chemistry { Theory / Practical	...	83
Drawing	...	32
Needlework		
Cookery	...	
Music	... ...	
TOTAL %	... ...	59.0

Position for Term (a) Examination... *6*

(b) Form ... *13*

Position for Year (a) Examination ... *16*

(b) Form ... *7*

Weekly Position in Form	14	10	10	14	11	12	10	6	17	14		

Number of times absent — Morning ... *6* Afternoon ... *6*

" " late — Morning ... *0* Afternoon ... *1*

Conduct, etc.

Conduct Very good.
A good and uniform position
maintained. *W.S. Fairbrother.*

Headmaster.

Next Term commences ... *Sept 9th 1919*

Parents are requested to preserve these Reports and submit two or three when the pupil is applying for a situation.

John Greenhalgh's school report in 1919. (Joan Anderson – Ladybridge WI)

'I was born in 1908 at a farm in Mellor. At eleven years old I had to take my two brothers to school. We walked two miles with a basket and a large basin full of cold rice pudding, two dishes and three spoons. At dinnertime we went to the mill yard for hot water so we would have a drink of tea, and we just sat on the hot pipes and ate our rice pudding.' *(Annie Pilkington – Hapton WI)*

▣ LEYLAND METHODIST SCHOOL 1935 ▣

'I started at Leyland Methodist school in 1935 when I was almost five years old. The reception class teacher welcomed me and I felt at home immediately.

We were in a small narrow room where we were taught letters and numbers, using chalk on slates. At playtime we were each given a small beaker of hot Horlicks.

The school buildings were purely functional, nobody had made any attempt to construct buildings of beauty. When new rooms were needed they were built of brick or wood or whatever was available. The toilets were outside in a block of brick with an undercover passageway. This was a perfect place for us to play "chasing".

I admit to remembering playing in the yard more than I remember the lessons. The year went in seasons. It was skipping rope time, or top and whip time, then it might be marbles or playing ball up against the plentiful walls. We played tig. I remember tiggy hand out, and chain tig. I loved all this because as an only child I had no play-mates at home.

In school we progressed from small chairs and tables to big wooden desks for two with seats attached, from chalk and slates to pencil and paper and then to pen and ink. It was somebody's job to fill the ink-well's every Monday morning, and to give out the blotting paper.

A big event in the school week was a trip to the school clinic. This was two terraced houses joined into one on Hastings Road, Leyland. It had a dark green shiny floor and smelled strongly of disinfectant. The school nurse reigned there. She was called Nurse Hughes and she wouldn't stand any nonsense. We sat patiently in the dark green waiting room till called for. We went

Marjorie in 1940, a pupil at Leyland Methodist school. (Marjorie Acton – Clayton-le-Woods WI)

upstairs to see the school dentist and straight on to see the optician. I don't think that even Nurse Hughes realised that some of us learned the letters on the eye testing chart before going in to see the doctor. We thought that not to be able to see them was something of a disgrace.

Whilst I was at this school the war started so we had gas mask drill, and practised rushing out to the air raid shelter which was about five minutes away at the far end of Brook Mill field. That was fun, for we had a story or read comics, or sang whilst the teacher seemed to have a never-ending supply of sweets for us.'
(Marjorie Acton – Clayton-le-Woods WI)

▣ SCHOOL AT HOOLE ▣

'Education for village children in the late 1930s and early 1940s began at five years and continued at the same school until the age of 14, unless you were one of the fortunate few who won a scholarship to a grammar school at the age of eleven or had parents who could afford grammar school fees.

Apart from the first days it was most unusual for mothers to escort children to and from school; if there were no older sisters or brothers the custom was to ask a "big girl" from the top class if she would generally take care of the little one. It was considered an honour to have this responsibility.

After infant class, school was very disciplined. Several school years would be taught together in one classroom by the same teacher and the lessons were after morning assembly and prayers. Scripture was followed by arithmetic, then it would be playtime.

Milk monitors would bring in crates of milk containing third-pint bottles for which we paid 2½d per week and drank with a straw pushed through a hole in the cardboard top. These tops when washed were excellent for making woollen pom-poms.

After a play outside it was back to lessons, reading, English or composition. At twelve o'clock dinner time, most children went home but those living some distance took sandwiches and drank water from the drinking fountain in the cloakroom. Afternoon lessons were more varied – history, geography, drawing, nature study, craft, needlework, singing and games. Boys over eleven years had woodwork lessons half a day each week at Longton school where they had a specially equipped room, and older girls went there, too, one day every fortnight for cookery in winter and for laundry in summer.

We wrote with simple pens, a nib fitted into the holder. The nibs had to be changed frequently as they became cross-legged. The ink was mixed with powder, terrible stuff, especially when pupils pushed bits of blotting paper through the hole in the ink well.' *(Eileen Harrison – Hoole WI)*

❖ TABLES AND CANES ❖

'My first school was a mile and a half's walk from home, the latter part through open meadow and parkland. My most vivid memory is of playing in the hay and jumping on the haycocks, coming home from school at haytime. Of course the sun way always shining!

This was a country school and most pupils had to walk across fields to reach it. Many children therefore wore clogs. I longed for a pair and eventually my mother gave in and bought me a pretty pair of clogs in brown leather with "gold" studs, but no clog irons, so I couldn't made sparks with them in the playground.

Just before we moved away into another county for several years, I was "put up" at the age of six. This class contained three age groups and the teacher believed that "sparing the rod spoiled the child". None of her pupils was going to be spoiled!

Each morning we had to stand round the classroom walls for "tables". Every child was asked a question after we had chanted together "once two is two, two twos are four" etc. How dreadful it was if we got a hard one like 8 times 7 or 12 times 11! Woe betide those who could not answer or gave a wrong answer. Out came the cane and they received a stroke on each hand.

The teacher believed that boys were totally uncivilised, girls slightly less so. Each boy had to share a desk with a girl, much to the disgust of both. Some benches took three and then the girl was placed in the middle. Twenty years later I was to marry the boy who sat in the desk behind me and tugged my long hair mercilessly.' *(Vera Proctor – Hapton WI)*

The start of the school holiday to Norfolk in 1946, taken on the village green at Eccleston. (Maureen Wane – Eccleston WI)

❖ DINNER MONEY ❖

'I grew up in the small Lancashire mill town of Westhoughton and from 1950 to 1954 attended the local primary school. When I was in the top class (Primary 6) the headmistress, Miss Ashton, asked another girl, Mary Hargreaves and me if we would carry out a task for her every Thursday lunchtime. This involved eating our school dinner quickly and then collecting from the staff room a brown shopping bag in which was an envelope containing the whole school's dinner money collected that morning. We had to walk about a mile to the butcher's in Market Street where we handed over the envelope and sometimes were given notes in exchange; other times we had to tell Miss Ashton that the butcher would "sort it out at the weekend".

We then walked back to the school just in time for afternoon lessons. I suppose we were picked for this task because we seemed "sensible girls" or did Miss Ashton see an early affinity for money – I am now treasurer of Ainsdale WI! (*Joan Burgess – Ainsdale WI*)

THE WORLD OF WORK

On the Land

Farming was a way of life for many people in Lancashire. Life on the land has changed so much, but many of us can recall when horses provided the only power and harvest time brought hard work and celebration.

▨ Hiring Time ▨

'In 1919 my father bought a farm in the Lancaster area, where his family had lived for many years. Farmers hired a lot of men in those days before mechanisation. There were hiring fairs at Whitsuntide and Michaelmas. Young people of 14 years of age would be hired to work on the farms for six months at a time, often staying for several years. My grandfather's farm had an "out kitchen" where the men had their meals, with bedrooms above where they slept.' *(Norah Hargreaves – Overton & District WI)*

'The 22nd of June saw the hiring of Irish men at Bentham; they came for the hay month and then went on to potato picking. Many times the hay was not finished by the time the month was up if it had been a wet period. In the 1920s and 1930s there was hiring at Ulverston, at Martinmas and Whitsuntide, when farmers went to hire workers for the farms, a lot of them coming from the Barrow and Askam areas. This custom ended during the war.' *(Ethel Stephenson – Over Kellet WI)*

▨ The Pattern of Farm Life ▨

'Before 1940 farming was a very labour-intensive occupation. The whole family had to undertake milking and all the jobs in the fields. Our new farm at Outwood, near Radcliffe was larger than our old home and more horses were bought to undertake the spring ploughing and sowing. Root crops required hoeing

John Wane of Eccleston in the early 1900s – the door is specially shaped to enable a mare in foal to pass through. (Maureen Wane – Eccleston WI)

Marjorie, her father Len and two prisoners of war, Karl and Adolf, who helped on the farm in the 1940s. (Marjorie Engmann – Stoneclough WI)

and thinning – backache and blisters were common.

The lovely smell of new-mown grass heralded the start of haymaking. The swathes would be turned several times to dry before being raked into rows and eventually heaped into haycocks by labourers using pitchforks and rakes. The dried hay would then be loaded on to carts and taken to be stacked in the barn for winter fodder.

The swish of the scythe as the farmer cut a path round his cornfield ready for the binder to start cutting marked the start of harvest. Labourers would follow the binder, stacking the sheaves into stooks to dry. The individual stooks placed in neat rows around the field were left to dry for several days before being loaded on to waggons and the intricacies of building a corn stack were taught to me by my grandfather, for everyone had to help at harvest time.

The back-breaking job of potato picking was the beginning of the autumn harvest, when local women would come to help

THE WORKERS EMANCIPATION

It is rather hard that an old man should have to find his way to the gates of the tomb bleeding and footsore through the brambles and thorns of poverty.

We are cutting a new path — a longer, an easier, a pleasanter one through fields of waving corn

The Chancellor of the Exchequer, at Limehouse July 30th 09 & the People's Budget.

VOTE for HELME

Published by the Political Committee of the National Liberal Club, London, S.W., and Printed by Ideas & Illustrations, 130, Fleet St., I

An invitation to a Liberal election meeting at Arkholme in 1910, calculated to appeal to farm labourers at a time when the threat of the workhouse loomed at the end of a lifetime of hard work. (Emily Hacking – Leck & Cowan Bridge WI)

with the picking. Turnips, swedes and mangolds were next to be harvested. These were pulled by hand, topped and tailed using a good sharp knife, then left in heaps ready to be loaded and taken to the farm for storage for winter cattle food.

During the winter months repairs were usually undertaken, fencing and gates repaired, hedges cut and laid, shippons and outbuildings whitewashed. The days before Christmas were spent plucking and dressing chickens, ducks and geese ready for the festivities.

In really bad winters we would be snowed up and have to deliver milk by sledge. Sometimes surplus milk had to be tipped down the drain if the milk wagon failed to get through the snow.

On any farm the kitchen was a focal point, a meeting place for the many travellers and craftsmen who called. There would always be a welcome drink and home-made scone for them. The wonderful aroma of baking permeated the air as my mother made her bread, pies and cakes on the old kitchen table. We had to be self-sufficient as there was no corner shop. Meals were plain but nourishing, rabbit and partridge were very often on the menu as Dad would go out shooting. Cooking and baking was on the old kitchen range and we had no electricity.

This was the general pattern of farm life until the Second World War started. The need to produce food for the nation made farming a vital occupation and every spare acre was ploughed to produce food. Tractors and modern machines replaced the horses and the whole farming structure quickly changed. Subsidies were available to farmers for lime and fertilisers and each farm was instructed how many acres of potatoes and cereal crops they must grow by the War Agricultural Committee.

Food rationing was introduced for everyone but extra rations were always available for farmers at harvest and threshing times. We were never short of a few eggs, or potatoes could always be "exchanged" for luxuries!' (*Marjorie Engmann – Stoneclough WI*)

▣ THRESHING TIME ▣

'In the 1940s threshing took place in the short days of winter, the giant thresher being driven by an enormous steam engine. Every farmer at Hoole took his turn to have his corn threshed. The thresher was driven as close as possible to the stack or bay in the barn. The thresher man usually brought a team of men with him. The sheaves were handed, one by one, to a man on top of the machine who cut the strings and let the oats or wheat slide into a moving drum that separated the chaff from the ears of corn, the straw going on to be baled. The precious corn was bagged and weighed by the farmer himself. Chaff came down a chute into bags between the machine and the stack behind. The men had only 18 inches to work in. These bags had to be changed when full and then they would be put in a shed to be used for winter bedding.

Try to imagine a winter's day, usually raining, with black smoke, choking dust and hissing steam all around, the noise of the engine with moving parts and unguarded pulleys just inches

Baggin' time in the cornfield, 1940. The sheaves were gathered into stooks of six or eight and left to dry out before being stored for later threshing. If it rained they all had to be fluzzed (shaken out!). (Lilian Ainscough – Scarisbrick WI)

from your face, then you will have some idea of the scene. At noon everyone went into the farmhouse for dinner – usually a hotpot or home-cured ham, followed by apple pie or rice pudding washed down with pint mugs of tea. The men came in just as they worked, covered in oil, chaff and sweat. There was always good-humoured banter at the table but they were all keen to get back and finish the job. As the stack got lower the men put netting round to prevent rats and mice escaping – the young men on the stack having great sport. At last the steam engine shuddered to a stop and all was finished. The engine and thresher went their stately way to the next farm and we were left to clear up the yard and count the result of the harvest.' *(Hoole WI)*

◈ THE POTATO HARVEST ◈

'I must have been about eleven years old when, in 1919, volunteers were asked for at my school, St Saviour's at Bamber

Winter in the early 1930s and time to open the potato clamps. The man on the left is lifting the potatoes out with a wooden shovel, onto a stand with a hand riddle on top which will sieve out the earth and small potatoes (used for animal feed). Large potatoes go into the bagging box and then into a hundredweight sack, which is stitched closed. The sacks will be carted to the railway goods yard and sent to market. (Lilian Ainscough – Scarisbrick WI)

Bridge, for potato picking at Cuerden Hall. I went with six boys and two other girls for a month, one week in the morning and the next in the afternoon with school lessons during the other half of the day.

We all walked together along the Wigan Road and down Shady Lane to the entrance to Cuerden Hall, owned in those days by Mr R. A. Tatton. We never thought anything about walking so far by ourselves. We reported to the head gardener, Mr Bradley, and he took us to the potato field. We picked by hand, of course, filling buckets before the potatoes were thrown into big containers. The potatoes were being grown on the estate because of the shortages of food during the war. My mother would walk over the fields to get some from a farm if she heard they were available.' *(Ida Grime – Clayton le Woods WI)*

CROOK FOLD FARM

'Nowadays the Bradshaw and Harwood area is a thriving suburb of Bolton, but when I was a child it was far more rural, based mostly on farming and with much of the industry coming from two bleachworks – one now forms part of a prestigious housing development and the other has disappeared completely to become part of a local park. Many of the fields that once grew crops are covered now with homes for growing families instead.

At Crook Fold Farm were the Hulmes – father, mother and two sons – all with farming in their blood. Both Mr and Mrs Hulmes were the children of farmers and knew no other life. Their farm was mostly devoted to livestock, milking herds generally, though during the war some fields were used for crops.

Mr Hulmes (Percy senior) was a strong man who knew his craft and how to strike a good bargain. His workers knew him to be fair and reasonable – a good day's pay for a good day's work. The Irish labourers would say, "He's a grand man, but the Missis – she's another matter!" Mrs Hulmes (Annie) was the "power behind the plough", you might say. She was a real character, small in height but strong and tireless, becoming, as she grew older, wider and wider about the hips and shoulders until she seemed almost square in shape. Nevertheless, she had been very pretty in her younger days and there was something about her even when she was an old woman.

Annie lived and breathed the farm. It was a prosperous establishment, but to Annie, spending money on labour-saving devices was a waste. She had no time for washing machines or hoovers – "What's wrong with scrubbing and sweeping?" she would ask. Nor did she waste money on clothes. Her usual uniform was an old blouse and skirt, and perhaps a cardigan if there was a blizzard blowing, the whole covered with an old apron, and a mob cap on her head. She always wore clogs, indoors and out.

Day's end at Crook Fold Farm and time to wash – outside, of course, with no running water laid on. (Rita Hulmes – Bradshaw & Harwood WI)

Sadly, her husband died quite young, but she was determined the farm would not suffer. Young George, then aged 19, virtually took over, but Annie was always there making sure everyone worked. Farmhands knew no slacking would be allowed. It was a sight to behold to see Annie berating a large, red-faced Irish worker, almost double her height, until he was forced to admit that he had not quite worked a full ten hours or whatever it was, because she had seen him resting on his fork for more time than it needed to get his breath back. However, after winning the argument she would usually relent and pay the fair rate.

"She's a divil, that woman, but a fair one," they had to admit. They knew they could not pull the wool over her eyes, but they also had to admit she fed them well. The old farmhouse kitchen, with its flag stone and ancient range, would see her producing vast meat pies, immense pans of potatoes and vegetables, and more often than not, rice pudding. Nothing was quite like her rice pudding, made with the rich milk her cows produced.

Crook Fold Farm now forms part of the park and a new golf course. The old farm buildings where Annie ruled are used as the clubhouse.' (*Rita Hulmes – Bradshaw & Harwood WI*)

IN THE MILLS

Many children went straight from school into the mills, and in many families it was a case of following in father's, or mother's, footsteps.

⬛ IN THE MILL AT BLACKBURN ⬛

'My aunt Catherine was born in Blackburn in 1913. Her mother died in childbirth, so she and her sister Janey were brought up by their father Walter with the help of his sister.

When she was 14, Catherine went to work in the mill with her sister. When I was talking to her about this I was surprised to learn that she worked for the first six months without pay. Her father had to pay one of the experienced weavers to train her. She worked Monday to Friday from half past seven until half past five with an hour for dinner. Saturdays were worked from half past seven until twelve o'clock. Saturday was part of the working week. So at 14, Catherine was working 49½ hours a week for nothing.

Dinner was usually taken to work, maybe hotpot or sausage and mash. Before dinner time this was taken and put in the works oven to heat up. Tea was brewed usually from an urn near the oven and drunk from a gill pot by the women or a kit by the men. Catherine and Janey, with the rest of the workers, ate their dinner by their looms and sat either on a wooden box or a tin can that had held weft for the loom. After dinner they sometimes went for a walk to look at the nearby shops.

They had to buy their own overalls and change from shoes into clogs before they started work. They wore black woollen stockings but nothing on their heads. During the war when

Mary Davenport working in the weaving shed at Alec Barlow's Mill, Edenfield in the 1930s. The mill is no longer in existence. (Gladys Hughes – Hapton WI)

women adopted the "Veronica Lake" hairstyle, which was long hair hanging over one eye, and accidents began to happen, safety was looked at and women started wearing turbans.

The mills were very noisy and people had to shout to make themselves heard. Catherine did not lip read very well, though Janey was good at it. A good lip reader could tell what someone was saying at the other end of the shed. Many of the weavers of this era became very deaf.

The mills were sometimes very damp, though this was not the case in Catherine's first mill. The overlooker, or tattler as he was called, had to be told if something went wrong and hopefully he repaired it. If there was a "mash", the shuttle caught and all the ends broke and it had to be pieced so it didn't show. Anything flawed had to be bought by the weaver herself so she would go amongst her workmates and raffle it to help pay for it. People helped each other, so if they could they would join in the raffle.

Weft had to be collected from the "weft place" in another part of the factory and Catherine would ask the weaver nearest to watch her loom while she was away as they were left running all the time. The cloth carrier collected the finished cloth which was folded and put on a truck and taken to the warehouse to be checked for flaws. From there it went to be finished and sometimes dyed.

Only a few men were weavers, the majority being women. Children were usually looked after by Grandma or Auntie, the extended family was the norm in those days. Very occasionally a neighbour was paid to look after a child.

At Christmas, if the boss was in a good mood, the engines were stopped for an hour to allow for a party to be held. There was no canteen in the factory so all year they would pay into a Christmas club, then at Christmas someone would organise the food. There would be boiled ham and cheese sandwiches, meat pies, mince pies, trifle and tea. Catherine said, "The lads took the opportunity to go round kissing the girls." The mill closed for Christmas Day only and shut down on New Year's Day too.

In Blackburn, Wakes Week was the third week in July and it was holiday without pay. Most people went away, usually on days out with friends, Blackpool, Southport and Morecambe being popular. Catherine and Janey would go early in the morning with their sandwiches and buy a jug of tea on the beach, then fish and chips later for tea. The Pleasure Beach was visited and they always had a walk along the Promenade for a "blow", never mind the weather.' *(Kay Slater – Lea WI)*

❖ A Sad Time ❖

'At Read two cotton weaving mills, owned by Joseph Kemp, provided work for the villagers and several rows of stone-built houses were rented out to workers. A number of food shops were also kept busy by the mill workers; they would take their potato pie dish to the shop on their way to work and call for it, now ready-made to take home, for tea. When the cotton trade collapsed many families had to look elsewhere for work. It was a very sad time. Mr Kemp went bankrupt; he had given so much for the village.' *(Alice Dyson – Simonstone with Read WI)*

The weaving shed at Carrington & Dewhurst's Grove Mill, Eccleston in 1947. They wove parachute material here during the war and went on to weave nylon, becoming Carrington Viyella. Grove Mill is now an antiques warehouse. (Maureen Wane – Eccleston WI)

◈ IN THE FAMILY ◈

'Cotton weaving was the main industry in the 1920s and most families at Ramsbottom had employment in the mills. In those years parents stuck to the idea that if one member of the family went into the mill, all the rest did the same. My mother would have liked to be a teacher. She used to help at her school when a member of staff was absent, but when the head teacher went to see my grandmother to ask her permission for my mother to be trained, Grandma said that all her sisters were in the mill and she would have to do the same.' *(Beatrice Sellers – Greenmount Village WI)*

◈ THE BOBBIN MILL ◈

'Lancashire is, of course, known principally for its cotton mills, but in the Ribble Valley, where water was often used as power, corn mills and bobbin mills were most common. Hurst Green had one of the remaining, working bobbin mills within living memory, and during the Second World War, from about 1940 onwards when fewer men remained in the village, young women and girls went to work in the bobbin mill to do the work of the men.

Wooden bobbins were produced in Hurst Green and sent to the cotton mills in the nearby towns to be used for the production of cloth, khaki for uniforms. The wood was often felled locally, taken to the saw mill, then brought to the bobbin mill in lengths of about four foot on the back of a wagon. The young girls had to carry piles of these logs to the dry house – a shed with a furnace underneath fuelled by shavings from the mill floor. The work was hard and dirty, and young arms ached with the weight of the logs. It was the men's job to keep the furnace going by collecting the shavings. After a few days to dry out, the logs were sent back to the saw mill to be cut into eight inches lengths ready to be made into bobbins.

We worked from 7.30 in the morning until 5.30 at night, and Saturday mornings. Although we got an hour off for our dinner (when we generally came home) we were not allowed to stop for a tea break, tea was supped on the job. The foreman used to watch us all the time and if he felt there was too much chattering going on he'd

Hambledon Mill, Accrington and some of the girls who worked there in the 1920s. (Lucy Day – Barton WI)

make some unflattering comment to that effect, so that we quietened down. The work was physically demanding and tiring. We had to polish the completed bobbins by hand using wood shavings from the machines. Carrying the logs to the drying house produced many a bruise and cut, and blisters on hands and arms were common.

As we worked the machines, the shavings collected on the floor. There was a technique of sweeping the shavings to one side with your foot as you continued working the turner. Some of us never quite mastered the art! To relieve monotony and the noise we girls would sing all the latest popular songs, until the foreman could stand it no longer. Many a time we escaped to the lavatory, our only respite, to read a precious letter from our men at the front.

One of the worst aspects was walking home through the village, still in our overalls with shavings in our hair, past all the old men sitting on "The Monkey Rack" (a park bench) enjoying the afternoon air.' *(Jan Hardy – Hurst Green WI)*

OTHER WAYS WE MADE A LIVING

From kitting milk to life in an office, from the saddler to the blacksmith, there were many other ways we made our living.

▣ COFFINS AND CARTS ▣

'My father was a joiner, wheelwright and funeral undertaker. This trade is very different today. Then, coffins were always made by hand, and wood had to be stored and seasoned. Our coffin wood was always kept in the house cellar for a considerable time, the best being oak; pieces were then taken out and had to be bent into the shape and size required. The lids were made to fit with great precision, then they were polished and all the fittings put into position; name plates had to be engraved in the one day. Funeral arrangements were all personal through to the grave, cremations were very rare. Mother used to go out to assist in the preparation, measuring and other

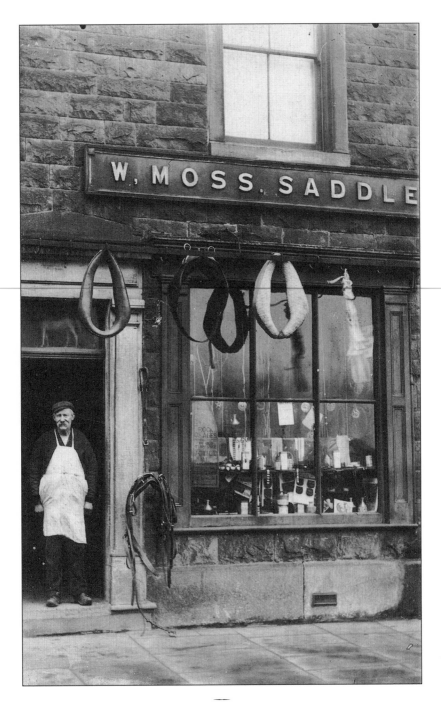

Moss's saddler's shop in Berry Lane, Longridge in the early 1900s. His son Herbert was also a saddler and had a hut in Warwick Street – 'it was absolutely full of leather – saddles, belts, straps, horse brasses, bits and pieces, and there was just a narrow way through to his bench where he sat on a high stool stitching with a "razzin" (resin) block beside him, through which the threads were drawn. He was a great craftsman and it made him very sad when leather began to be replaced by plastic.' (Mary Headley – Caton WI)

requirements, especially in the case of females. Before the motor hearse, black horses were used to pull the hearse to church; my dad always wore a tail coat and a silk top hat up until the 1950s.

Milk floats and horse-drawn carts were made on the premises, each business having their own style. They were usually made of ash and all made by hand. The "fellies" (the wood next to the iron rim on the wheel) were shaped for the rim of the wheel, the spokes being nicely shaped to fit into the hub. When assembled the whole wheel had to be put into the iron rim, which had been heated in a furnace, then was plunged into a well of water to enable the rim to shrink to fit tightly. The shafts were always made of spruce to allow for the bending, and when the carts were finished they were painted green and then a man would line all down the sides with a very fine brush, most professional.' *(Ruth Pearson – Clayton-le-Dale WI)*

◈ A HIGH CLASS GROCER ◈

'At the age of 15 I went after my first job, to a "high class grocer's", in Rochdale. "Eleven shillings a week and start at nine, half day on Tuesday and work until seven o'clock," my employer told me. Fortunately it was near to my home so I was able to come home for lunch. The proprietor's wife, Mrs Whitworth, was in charge of "our" branch and her husband had another establishment in the town centre.

We served all the big houses, lots of which kept foreign maids who used to ring up and give the orders. I sometimes answered the phone on the wall and got very confused as I couldn't understand their accents. Come to think of it, we hardly ever saw the best customers, as they had their orders delivered.

There was Kenneth, a boy a few years older than me, and young George, the errand boy, who used to go out in all weathers on his bike with a big basket on the front and cheered us up no end with his whistling and his jokes.

Nothing was too good for the customer. "Mr Hunter likes his bacon cut on number five and he has it smoked for his breakfast on Sunday," said Mrs Whitworth. "You must place each slice so one overlaps the other, and it will look nice when it is opened."

Sometimes a "maiden" lady would call in on her afternoon walk and order some special blended tea, which we kept in big cannisters on the shelf, or a tin of Ronuk polish. She insisted on having the tin wrapped up in brown paper and tied with string. I remember one day after doing this service for her she said, "Never mind, send the youth round with it." The "youth" being George. This made Kenneth laugh and poke fun at George and later, when Mrs Whitworth was in her quarters above the shop, they had a skirmish in the back.

We used the back of the shop for storage and some days we had to weigh out sugar into blue paper bags, and sometimes flour, which made us look very pale afterwards! I don't recall us having any break and I know I used to get very hungry. Sometimes I would smuggle a biscuit out of the glass-topped biscuit tins on display, ginger flavoured with lemon was my favourite. I would put it in my overall pocket and eat pieces when I thought she wasn't watching.

The worst times were during the freezing weather. "We must keep the shop door open," says tough Mrs Whitworth, "or they will think we are closed," and "Aren't the ferns made of the ice beautiful on the windows?" We were on a corner so we got the wintry blast from both directions and when I went home for lunch I used to huddle over the coal fire and nearly fall asleep. Of course, heating of any kind in the shop was nil in those days of no refrigeration, the perishable food was more important than mere shop assistants.' *(Vera Walls – Bradshaw & Harwood WI)*

▦ Kitting Milk ▦

'Every Saturday and Sunday in the 1940s, and most of my school holidays I was expected to lend a hand with the milk round – no six-day week in those days, milk was delivered seven days a week and Christmas Day was no exception.

We had two Shire horses called Daisy and Robin and a very smart float which was painted, grained and varnished. Most dairy farmers had great pride in the smartness of their turnout. We carried two large kits of milk, a 10 gallon and a 13 gallon, with a ladle for measuring out which hooked on the side of the kit. We also had several smaller kits, one and two gallons besides gill, pint and quart kits. We did bottle some milk but as I remember only about a couple of crates. The bottle tops were made of waxed cardboard.

The horse was so familiar with the milk round it knew where to go and when to stop. Where cobbled streets were too steep for the horses we used to carry the milk in one or two gallon kits and ladle it out into the jug hopefully ready on the doorstep – and woe betide us if we spilt some on newly stoned steps! I took us all morning to deliver the milk, probably about four hours – longer at weekends as we had to knock for the money.

A pint of milk cost about 4½d at that time. Most customers

Edwin Cooper (second from left) worked as a door to door tea salesman for the Belfast & British Tea Company based in Preston. His round included Burnley, Nelson and Hapton. 'We lived in Latham Street in the Avenham area, in a terraced house belonging to the company, near to the offices and warehouse. Members of the family firm were addressed as Mr Alf and Mr Clifford.' (Rene Ibison – Lea WI)

The saddler's shop at Pilling in the 1920s – 'the hub for local news and gossip'. L. to r. are William Hornby, William and John Thornton (the saddlers), and Jim Porter. (Edith Robinson – Cabus WI)

were very friendly and certain ones were regular stopping places, where we were assured of a drink or a couple of newly baked cakes. Kitting milk, as we called it, was I suppose pleasant enough in summer, though I must say I don't think I was a very willing helper. Rain was another matter, no shelter in a horse and float and only a wet seat to sit on. Snow was even worse and quite hazardous. I'm sure the poor horse thought so too.' *(Dorothy Devereux – Gt Harwood & District WI)*

❖ AT THE SADDLER'S ❖

'One of the things we liked to do as children was to go to watch Dad at work. He and Grandad were the village saddlers, a busy and thriving business then. Their workshop was a wooden shed opposite Pilling station.

There was a coke-burning stove in the centre of the shed and we loved to slice and cook potatoes on the top. There were always several old men sitting on the forms and this was the hub for the local news and gossip. There was great interest when the train came in; they all went outside to watch who had been "gadding off" and if there was someone they didn't know there was great speculation as to who it could be and who they would be visiting. They usually found out too. It was a very rare thing to see a stranger in Pilling then, as there were no buses and very few cars.

Dad and Grandad wore thick leather aprons and sat at high benches making and repairing horse collars and saddles etc. Harness and brasses hung on the walls and big rolls of ribbon, used for making decorations for horses for May Day and shows. Two of my great-uncles had horse-drawn traps and a landau for hire and one of my first memories of Garstang is of coming to a brass band contest in one of their traps. We jolted along for hours at almost walking pace. That must be 80 years since; I was almost five at the time. I still love the smell of leather which brings back happy memories.' *(Edith Robinson – Cabus WI)*

▣ MASTER FARRIER AND BLACKSMITH ▣

'I was born in 1916, the seventh child in a very happy family of eleven children. Father was one of a long line of master farriers and blacksmiths and ran a busy smithy, at Cross Mill, near Scorton, employing an assistant until my eldest brother was old enough to help. The day began with lighting the furnace. The bellows for this purpose stood about five foot high and were manually operated with a long handle. Alongside the hearth was a stone water trough for cooling the iron as required.

It was not unusual to see a few farmers waiting their turn to have their horses shod or small parts of machinery repaired, as telephones were unheard of. One of the seasonal jobs was making metal hoops and hooks for local children. They were grand for running the couple of miles to school.' *(Phyllis Gifford – Chipping WI)*

▣ AT THE OFFICE ▣

'I was always grateful to my mother for keeping me at school until I was 17 and had passed the matriculation exam, but of course there was no hope of going on to university as this was the 1930s when there were so many out of work and conditions were much worse than they are today, with very little help from the Government.

I left school on Thursday and started work on the Monday, having obtained the job by answering a newspaper advertisement. The firm was an old-established family concern which made parts of railway engines, and I was among the first women to be employed by them. Besides me there was a woman secretary and several were given jobs in the foundry. The men all resented us at first but were always kind and respectful.

I was the last to leave at 5.30 pm when I took the letters, after stamping them, to the post office, so it was 6 pm or later when I caught the tram partway home. I was paid 12s 6d per week, 10s for my mother and 2s 6d for me, from which I paid my fares and bought my stockings. Silk stockings were sixpence a pair from Woolworths but they laddered very easily and I had to buy at least one pair a week.

I was glad when the director had a visitor because when I served them with tea some would leave a tip, sometimes a shilling. One who came twice a year used to leave half a crown, riches indeed, because I could go dancing or to the cinema for sixpence. (*Doris Darlington – Little Thornton WI*)

⚅ IN SERVICE ⚅

'I left home by train at the age of 14, with my case and a bunch of flowers for my future employer, sitting terrified on the edge of my seat. At Bolton I was met by Mr Bullough, who owned the Paragon Dress House. On arrival at his house, the brasses were waiting on the kitchen table ready to be cleaned.

I did all the household tasks – cooking and cleaning – for 7s 6d a week. Out of that I had to keep myself in black stockings, buy a postal order and stamp and send the rest home.

After two years I left Bolton. I was homesick and had no social life at all. I returned home and got a job as upstairs-downstairs maid at the house of the Coroner, Mr Holding, in Queen Square, Lancaster. I had no cooking to do here as a cook was employed, but I still had all the other jobs, including waiting on table.'
(*Margaret Sanderson & Marian Rigg – Bolton-le-Sands WI*)

Horrockses, Crewdson & Co. Ltd's sales office at Preston in 1950. The office was converted from a weaving shed and was freezing cold in winter and too hot in summer because of the glass roof. About 50 people, including typists and comptometer operators, worked in this noisy open-plan office. (Nancy Gough – Hoghton WI)

'Parkbridge was a small industrial village in the 1930s, with the ironworks at its centre. There were four rows of workers' cottages, about 40 in all, and six larger, bay-windowed houses for the managers, as well as a school, church and two chapels, five small farms, and a very grand manor house where the ironmaster lived.

In 1928 there was a great occasion in the village when Henry Ford came from America and took away our Newcomen engine (known as "Fairbottom Bobs"). It had been used for pumping water from the small coal and cannel mines, of which there were many in the area.

As children we played round the lamp at night or played ball against the house wall, and watched the men working in the ironworks through an iron grille. They rolled out the iron pigs into long lengths for the little steam engine, *Pegasus*, to take up to the main railway line. It was lovely and warm on cold winter evenings, and the men would throw sparks up at us from their red-hot tongs.' *(Mavis Defley – Fairbottom WI)*

WAR & PEACE

THE GREAT WAR
1914–1918

While the fighting took place far away, life at home was not easy and shortages of food and labour made themselves felt. Tragedies touched every town and village in the county.

◨ LIFE ON THE LAND ◨

'Memories are made of so much. The Great War of 1914 to 1918 made its impact on country children through knowing of young men from the farms "joining up" and appearing in khaki. Some came home at the end of the war and some did not. One mother lost two of her sons. Tragedy struck another family in our small community when a particularly severe form of influenza caused the death of a young mother in 1918. Her baby lived and her husband survived the dangers of the war.

Shortage of labour on the land was made up by daughters putting on trousers (such a phenomenon we children had not seen before, as those were the days when children could cling onto Mother's skirts). These be-trousered land girls tended cattle, worked in the hay field, drove a horse-drawn reaper – all the tasks done usually by the men of the family. Another source of help was from Bowerham Barracks, Lancaster, where soldiers recovering from wounds and not fit for combatant duties were available for farm work.

At the beginning of the war horses were requisitioned but as the Army became mechanised, happily there was little further need for horse power.

Living on the land made life easier for country people. There were whinberries and blackberries for the picking, mushrooms to be gathered and the produce of the farm garden and orchard. Mothers learned the art of bottling fruit when it was plentiful. This was continued between the wars and in the Second World War was supplemented by communal jam-making – on primus

Women took over many jobs formerly done by men during the First World War; this photograph of a postlady was taken in Liverpool. (Joyce Simm – Crag Bank WI)

stoves in a school room which, then, had no electricity supply. Canning of fruit was another skill. In view of expected rises in prices, eggs were preserved in waterglass.

In Fylde villages samphire, which grew on the marshes, was picked as a relish. The turf cart made a regular round in the same village when housewives would buy squares of turf (peat) with which to bank up their open fires.

Land, garden and home provided simple remedies. Every child knew that a dock leaf rubbed on a nettle sting would soothe the irritation. Wasp and bee stings needed the application of mother's blue bag. Goose grease was rubbed on weak chests and an egg beaten with milk and flavoured with rum helped to build up strength and restore an appetite. Honey, butter and lemon mixed were given for sore throats, followed by the application of a black woollen stocking wound round the throat of the sufferer to sleep in. An infusion of blackcurrant jam in hot water was a comfort to one feeling the effects of a bad cold. A severe case of whooping cough is said to have been cured by crushing wild garlic plants, putting them in a calico bag from which they exuded a strong odour and hanging the bag round the patient's neck to rest on the chest through the night and possibly the day too. An infusion of comfrey was used for sprains as was also comfrey oil. About the year 1915 people were still talking of the use of leeches in a case of pneumonia.' *(Jennett Fowler – Ulnes Walton WI)*

▣ DANGER FROM MUNITIONS ▣

'I remember the explosion at the munitions factory at White Lund, Morecambe in 1917. The sky was lit up for miles around and people were terrified. The houses in Bolton-le-Sands were evacuated in the middle of the night and people walked to safer, higher ground in Nether Kellet. I was too small to walk so I was pushed in a wheelbarrow already occupied by my grandfather, who had only one leg.' *(Hilda Storey – Bolton-le-Sands WI)*

WITH
FOND GREETINGS

FROM A
MUNITION
WORKER

HELPING
TO
"CARRY ON"

ON WAR SERVICE

THIS BADGE proves
I'm A "WORKER"
Who can ne'er be
dubbed a "shirker,"
And my output proves
that I have put on speed,
So with pride my Badge
I'll wear
To prove I do my share—
For Country, and the Lads,
when they're in need.

A postcard sent to Carnforth in 1917 – munitions work could be extremely dangerous. (Emily Hacking – Leck & Cowan Bridge WI)

THE SECOND WORLD WAR
1939–1945

*J*ust *20 years later, we were again facing shortages and rationing, while air raids became an everyday danger.*

❖ THE AIR RAIDS STARTED ❖

'Sunday, 3rd September 1939 at 11 am. We heard the announcement on the wireless by Mr Neville Chamberlain, the Prime Minister – "We are at war with Germany." What would that mean? Two days later my younger sister and two brothers were evacuated to relatives near Kirkby Lonsdale. My father had decided that I was old enough to help at home in the family business of producing and supplying fresh milk to the people of Bootle. We kept about 15 cows in the shippon and lived alongside the Liverpool to Southport railway line near the Alexandra Dock in Strand Road.

All the schools were closed. Most of the schoolchildren had gone to new homes in Southport with teachers, supposedly until the cessation of hostilities. Some of us who stayed at home went to St Mary's school to have lessons with the curate, Mr Wright. I remember how bored we were with "Architecture", being told about the types of doors and windows in castles, cathedrals and other ancient buildings.

Blackout curtains had to be fitted to windows, street lights remained unlit and vehicle headlamps dimmed so that no lights would be visible to enemy aircraft that may have got past the big silvery barrage balloons that were sited all over Merseyside as deterrents. Enemy aircraft always carried out their air raids on bright moonlit nights when the many railway lines would shimmer and look like never-ending snakes stretching for miles away from the river and docks.

The docks were dotted with those ships that had got past the U-boats in the Atlantic Ocean to bring our vital food supplies on which we were wholly dependent. Unfortunately many ships were sunk with huge loss of life before reaching the Mersey base.

The air raids started on Liverpool in 1940. As soon as the sirens started wailing, usually about 7 pm, everybody left what they were doing to go to a shelter, either an Anderson shelter lowered about three feet down in the backyard, or the Morrison table shelter in the kitchen, or a brick-built communal shelter in the street.

Bootle had the unenviable distinction of being one of the most blitzed towns in the whole country for its size, especially during the Christmas blitz, 1940 and the May blitz in 1941. The first raid was during the night of 29th August 1940. The first bomb, an incendiary, was dropped on the gasworks but caused little damage. Heavier raids followed the next night when 16 high explosives were dropped causing five fatalities, and on successive nights the town was bombarded and house property suffered.

The next heavy raid was the night of 21st September, when in addition to widespread damage to houses, industrial areas suffered severely, principally through fires caused in timber yards by incendiary bombs, lighting up everywhere. There was the continual smell of burning and huge palls of smoke rising up to a red sky as firemen, aided by civilians, fought bravely to extinguish the many fires, making use of the miles of hosepipes supplying water. Both the overhead railway, known as the Dockers' Umbrella, and Liverpool/Southport railway lines were damaged and had to be closed.

Gas and water mains were damaged, churches and chapels and schools were demolished and there was extensive loss of life, especially in the earlier part of the evenings when the raids started before people had arrived home from work. After one incident some injured people were put in an ambulance which was bombed on its way to hospital. These casualties were transferred to another ambulance which drove into a newly formed crater and were eventually wheeled into hospital on a handcart amid falling bombs and the hiss of flying shrapnel.

Thousands of ration books were lost when the Food Office was damaged by fire. One of the greatest tragedies was the deaths of devoted WVS members who perished when St Andrew's Hall, being used as a Rest Centre to which they had transferred homeless citizens in their care, received a direct hit killing everyone, including a lot of my friends.

On 8th May 1941 the terrible destruction of the Co-op stores in Stanley Road resulted in the loss of 50 people who were trapped and killed in the underground shelter. This particular night saw the destruction of Bootle's only theatre – the famous Metropole, and the most macabre feature of this terrible night was the total destruction by fire of Marsh Lane Baths, being used as a mortuary.

The total casualties were 450 fatalities, 983 seriously injured and 443 slightly injured; 2,013 houses were totally destroyed and out of 17, 189 houses, those damaged amounted to 16,300. In all some 26,500 incidents of damage were recorded – some properties being damaged again and again.

Stirrup pumps in buckets of water and sandbags were always readily available in accessible places. The helmeted ARP wardens came round when there was a lull checking to see if help was needed.

Our shippon was damaged one night and the cattle (none were injured) were driven to other suitable premises, but unfortunately got tangled up in fallen and trailing electric wires across the streets.

My home was damaged and my parents and I, unable to sleep in our own beds upstairs, slept in the air raid shelter. We had a mattress on a raised platform but when it got too cold we slept in the kitchen on two armchairs and a sofa. I well remember the interest shown when a landmine was dropped, on a parachute. The mine did not explode and we children took pieces of the silk rope home, but eventually when the parachute was draped in the central library for everyone's attention it had to be removed before it finally melted away in the form of souvenirs.

When school did eventually start we were forbidden to use some of the buses because of shortages of petrol and the roads became impassable because of craters and rubble from fallen properties. Walking was the order of the day and no late arrivals at lessons.

Thomas Higginson in his Home Guard uniform, at Longlands Farm, Stalmine. The Home Guard brought together the old and young, and those in reserved occupations. (Barbara Briggs – Winmarleigh WI)

In 1945 the war in Europe ended and we all enjoyed our street parties despite food rationing. On VE Day my mother made all the custard. We all sat round tables down the middle of the street and had organised games and races. The love and friendship with neighbours was wonderful, everyone always helping somebody else.

How lovely it was to listen to the bells of those churches still left standing when they were allowed to ring at the cessation of hostilities. *(Maureen Gibson – Aspull & Haigh WI)*

❖ LIVERPOOL ABLAZE ❖

'I was 13 years of age when war was declared and lived in south Liverpool not too far from the river Mersey and the docks. I well remember the sirens, the bombing and particularly the May Blitz.

We had an Anderson shelter in the garden and my father fitted it with bunks and electricity. Most nights we had just gone to bed when the air raid siren sounded and we would sleepily make our way downstairs and into the shelter.

My home was on a corner and a big anti-aircraft gun, nicknamed "Big Bertha", was positioned there. When it was fired the ground shook and so did we! One night a landmine exploded nearby and the whole road had their windows blown out. We spent the rest of the war with boarded-up windows and the electric light permanently on. Many incendiaries were dropped, some in our garden. They lit up the whole area brilliantly and were almost as frightening as the real bombs.

I remember an incident when a bus taking workers to the plant where they built Halifax bombers was suddenly attacked by an evening plane. The driver zig-zagged all over the road but far from being afraid, the passengers craned out of the windows to watch the dogfight which ensued when one of our planes came to the rescue.

The most vivid memory is of being at a friend's house during the May Blitz. Her house stood quite high and we stood on the terrace watching Liverpool ablaze. It was like a giant firework display with the whole sky glowing. We lost all our major department stores that night but miraculously the Cathedral still stood proud.

The strange thing is, I don't ever remember being frightened, even though we had to walk home at night in the pitch black, something I wouldn't like to do today. Many walked under the overhead railway – the "Dockers' Umbrella" – to avoid being hit by shrapnel.' *(Jean Tweats – Claughton-on-Brock WI)*

▣ A SUSPICIOUS OBJECT ▣

'I was 16 in 1940 and lived at home with my parents, helping in the family greengrocery business in Liverpool. The man who kept the butcher's shop next door was a special constable and an air raid warden. One night he called over the fence that he was suspicious of an object in our front shop doorway. He thought it might be an incendiary device and he immediately evacuated the area and sent for the Fire Brigade and the Bomb Squad. It was in fact a hedgehog.' *(Peggy Moorcroft – Ainsdale WI)*

▣ MY INTERVIEW ▣

'I was born and bought up in Garstang, near Preston and can vividly remember standing on Dimples Lane canal bridge and seeing Liverpool lit up by incendiary bombs and with searchlights criss-crossing the night sky.

The nearest experience I had to bombing was one night when a German pilot became separated from his squadron and unloaded his bombs near Calder Vale. And then there was the horrendous day I was to spend in Liverpool for my interview at the office of one of the big banks.

It was my ambition to work at a bank in Preston and the appointed day came for my interview in Liverpool. The news on the wireless was that Liverpool had been badly damaged the night before and that no trains were running. It never entered my head to cancel the interview and, in any case, we didn't have a telephone. I caught the bus to Preston and found a long queue for the Liverpool bus. Many of the people were distressed because of the air raid.

My interview was in the afternoon but I arrived mid morning, had a look round the shops and had a cup of coffee. Then the horror started. The siren went and I was too frightened to go into a bomb shelter. Instead I went into a basement cafe which advertised itself as being bomb-proof.

I had the cheapest item on the menu, sausage and mash (1s 9d) and waited for the all clear. Twice more this exercise was repeated and yes, as I wasn't allowed to buy just a coffee, you've guessed it – I had sausage and mash twice more!

Remember, I was only a country girl and this was my first time alone in a big city. I was so frightened when the sirens were going that I thought that I would die on the spot. I prayed fervently to be spared and if that could be granted, I would be good for the rest of my life!

Eventually the time for my interview came and I made my way to the street where it was to be held. When I arrived the street was roped off and a policeman was standing there. "I want to go along this street," I said. "You can't," he said. "It has been bombed."

"But I have an interview at number . . . ," I said, expecting the building to arise magically before my eyes.

"You see that crater in the road? Those are the remains of the building you wanted. It no longer exists," said the policeman.

I turned and left not quite knowing what my feelings were. Sorry that it had been such a horrible day and glad that I could go home where, hopefully, my mother wouldn't give me sausage and mash for my evening meal.' *(Margaret Fisher – St Annes-on-Sea WI)*

◪ WARTIME IN SWINTON ◪

'I was seven and a half when war was declared. I lived with my parents and six year old brother in a semi-detached house in Swinton – five miles from Manchester. We had a large garden at the rear of the house – my parents' pride and joy where they spent many hours mowing the lawn and tending the flowers.

Early on in the war a huge hole was dug just outside the back door and into it went the Anderson shelter – soon covered with soil in an effort to hide its ugliness. Most of the rest of the garden was dug over to comply with the request to "Dig for Victory" and grow more food. My father built bunks in the shelter and shelves on which my mum kept the paraffin lamp and a large tin box in which was tea, sugar and biscuits – "in case"!

The first bombs to drop on Swinton were in August 1940 – all the windows were blown out of the Town Hall and then I realised what "the war" meant and the effect it could have on my friends and family. We went into the shelter on hearing the sirens, still in our night clothes but wearing our coats and carrying blankets, as we had done many times before. However, this night the bombs were so close and the noise so loud even our usual efforts of singing were not enough to cover the sound.

In the winter of 1940 an epidemic of diphtheria swept the area and I was one of those taken to the sanatorium for six weeks' isolation. I can remember seeing my parents looking at me through a window and wondering why they didn't come into the ward. I was one of the lucky ones, entirely due to my mum's insistence that my brother and I were in the first group in the Swinton area to be inoculated against the disease.

The worst of the bombing was at the time known as the "Manchester Blitz" in December 1940. It started on 19th December and went on until the 23rd. During the blitz a landmine landed on a street in Pendlebury killing 29 people and injuring over 50. The first night of the blitz the bombing went on for twelve hours and the following night for six hours. I can remember climbing the steps out of the shelter on the morning after the first night and looking towards Manchester. The whole sky was glowing and seemed to be on fire itself – and I was annoyed with my mum for not taking my brother and me to see the fires.

My father worked at the chloride factory making batteries for submarines and so was in a reserved occupation. He was in the ARP, too, so with working shifts and the ARP duties we didn't see much of him. One night during the blitz he came home with a "souvenir", a piece of an incendiary bomb that had come through the roof of the shed in which he was working, landing at his feet. He put it out with a bucket of sand standing nearby.

Later on the shelter became too damp to use and I can still remember the musty paraffin smell. As the raids became less frequent we stopped using it – instead we used to bed down under the kitchen table. This had two large folding leaves which nearly reached the floor. My mum draped thick blankets over the whole of the table and sides. She made a mattress from an old flock bed to go on the floor. My brother and I slept there quite happily, although we were woken by the sirens and during one heavy raid the vibration rattled the tins holding the gas masks which were hung on the back door knob. The cardboard boxes in which the gas masks had originally been issued had deteriorated and fallen apart and the tins were much more substantial. My mum was very relieved, though, to see that the criss-cross strips of sticky paper on the kitchen window had kept it intact.

There were more raids on Manchester in 1941 from January to October. The last raid on the city was on Christmas Eve, 1944, when 50 bombers flew over the Pennines from the East Coast, launching a stream of flying bombs on the area.

About 40 people had been killed in the Swinton area during the war-time bombing but through all the noise, disruption and horror of it I don't remember being afraid. This was because my parents never communicated their own anxieties and fears to my brother and I – and after all, Mr Churchill had assured us we would win the war.' *(Margaret Kershaw – Higher Walton WI)*

▣ IN THE SHELTER ▣

'As I remember, there was a wide variety of air raid shelters ranging from large, specially built communal shelters to accommodate whole neighbourhoods, to the Anderson shelter for individual families. Almost everything in between that could possibly be made suitable for the purpose was pressed into service – basements of large buildings, railway arches, underground stations etc. Our own shelter in south Manchester was in the cellar, which had been specially strengthened for the purpose.

In the early days of the war nothing very much happened apart from sporadic raids by the odd plane. In fact the media were beginning to call it the "phoney war", but in June 1940, after Dunkirk, the raids became more frequent. The almost nightly sounding of the sirens, always at about 7 pm, set the occupants of the four flats in our house trouping off to the cellar armed with flasks, hot water bottles, blankets, food and a pack of playing cards to occupy the long hours when sleep was impossible.

What a motley crew we were. We had an elderly widow lady prone to hysteria, a young wife whose husband was in the RAF, her brother who worked at a Royal Ordnance factory and who was convinced he was going to die (not from enemy action but from pneumonia after spending nights in a damp cellar), an Ethiopian gentleman, a relation of Haile Selassie and a fugitive from his own country, and my mother who suffered from acute arthritis and could not walk at all and had to be carried into the shelter. She must have been very frightened but I never heard her complain.

More often than not the playing cards were abandoned and the time was spent listening to the drone of the planes and the whistling of the bombs and speculating as to how near "that one" was. Then straining our ears for the welcome sound of the all clear. My 21st birthday was spent in the cellar but we still managed a celebration of sorts, someone produced a bottle of wine and a cake made of goodness knows what!

Then just before Christmas 1940 came the big one, the blitz on Manchester and Salford. The sirens sounded earlier than usual and the heavy and unremitting drone of the planes made us realise that this was no routine raid. The thud of the bombs and the shouts of the air raid wardens to anyone showing a light heralded a long, hard night. The flames from burning buildings as the incendiary bombs rained down lit the sky for miles around as the searchlights raked the sky trying to locate the enemy planes and the ack-ack guns added to the already deafening din.

I can still remember the eerie feeling when we crept outside during a lull to be met by a terrifying sight, debris everywhere. Our road was one of five running parallel and a stick of bombs had caught the other four in a direct line with our house but the only damage we suffered was the blowing out of the windows. It

Members of the Royal Observer Corps at their observation post at Longridge, high above the old quarries. One of them was local saddler Herbert Moss, who is remembered learning aeroplane silhouettes for identification purposes. (Mary Headley – Caton WI)

was almost daylight when the bombing ceased and the all clear sounded; what a long, long night it had been.

Next morning I set off to go to work, no one ever thought of taking a day off. There were no buses or trams running so I prepared myself for a walk of several miles to Salford where I worked for an engineering firm on essential war work. I picked my way through mounds of debris and broken glass and past faceless buildings, although some of the undaunted shopkeepers were trying to clear up the mess and open up their shops. Life had to go on and after all it was nearly Christmas and trade was important.

I eventually reached Salford and the dock area, past what had been terraces of neat houses with lace curtains and well donkey-stoned steps. Here the devastation was at its heartbreaking worst. Those houses still standing tottered dangerously and everywhere weary people, smoke begrimed and filthy, scrabbled amongst the remains of their homes trying to salvage what they could of their possessions, or even searching for loved ones.

Others were pushing their pathetic loads in prams or on handcarts to the temporary soup kitchens hastily set up in school halls or anything still standing. Here at least they could get a little comfort and refreshment for themselves and their tired, tearful, confused children and the old folk, that is if the standpipes were operating.

There followed many other raids on Manchester city centre where the mainly textile warehouses in Portland Street and Mosley Street burned furiously and popping in and out of air raid shelters became a way of life, but none left such an impression as that awful Christmas raid. Some time later while serving in the ATS I drove trucks taking ammunition to the rail heads and Southampton docks, often taking evasive action to dodge the doodlebugs, but this did not seem as terrifying as that one night listening to the continual crunch of the bombs landing and hoping after each one that it would be the last.' *(Joan Fenlon – Little Mitton WI)*

▣ A LOVELY AFTERNOON ▣

'One lovely Sunday afternoon, 27th October 1940, the sirens were sounded and we could hear and see a German plane overhead going towards Preston. A loud explosion was heard. A bomb had been dropped on a house in Ward Street, Lostock Hall and a whole family were killed – mother, father and six children, who had all been sheltering under the stairs. They were buried in Leyland parish churchyard. Altogether there were 24 people killed. The pilot had apparently been looking for Leyland Motors but missed the works.' *(Nellie Nelson – Lostock Hall WI)*

▣ NEAR ENOUGH ▣

'Holmeswood was far removed from the terrors of cities such as Liverpool which endured the terrible bombing raids. We had our air raid wardens and special constables who were quick to spot a chink of light through the blackout curtains and would ask you to get them adjusted – *quickly!* The fire watchers patrolled the lanes, equipped with stirrup pumps and buckets of sand on the look-out for incendiary bombs. The Home Guard trained at Burscough. Everyone who was fit and able took part in some way in local defence.

It was the local men of the National Fire Service who brought a measure of fame to Holmeswood. In a national competition for "a light trailer pump crew of four men", the Holmeswood team, having won through regional heats, were runners-up in the finals held in London.

There was great apprehension when two landmines were dropped on farmland in the village. Apart from broken windows and a huge crater where they fell – and one exploded – they did little damage. But one did not explode, so the area was cordoned off and all the people – and cattle – were evacuated. One elderly lady took a lot of persuading that it really was necessary for her to leave home. To us children there was a tinge of excitement about it all.

We were, however, near enough to Liverpool to be affected in another way. During the worst of the blitz people fled from the city in the early evening by whatever means they could. The trains on which we travelled home from school – Ormskirk to Rufford on the Liverpool–Preston line – were absolutely packed with women and their bewildered children. Some of them, arms in slings and bandaged, had already sustained injuries. Where they spent the nights we never knew. One group of people crowded into a furniture van belonging to a member of the group and drove to Holmeswood where they spent the evening in our village hall. Local people lent blankets to make them more comfortable and made cups of tea and soup. Another family was discovered trying to sleep in their car parked in a field gateway. The farmer took them home and they stayed in Holmeswood until the worst of the blitz was over.' *(Ellen Mee – Mere Brow & District WI)*

▣ A NIGHTMARE ▣

'It was one evening in August 1940, when my three babies were happily asleep in their cots. My husband and I had retired to bed when we heard planes droning overhead.

Suddenly we heard a crash and ran downstairs to find the room a blaze of fire. Two incendiary bombs had been dropped through the fanlight in the living room.

I ran upstairs and grabbed the twins and put them outside the front door, then ran back for the other child. I alerted my neighbours who looked after them while I ran back to help my husband with the stirrup pump we luckily had in our possession. The neighbours kept bringing buckets of water and I pumped like mad until we had the fire under control by the time the Fire Brigade came.

We had to vacate the house for three weeks until the damage was put right and it was safe to take the children back home. We were the only family in the road to get the bombs and to have such young children. It was a nightmare and a memory not to be forgotten.' (Gertie Simpson – Bolton-le-Sands WI)

▩ UNDER THE TABLE ▩

'I had just started at the secondary school in Darwen when the war began. By 1940 we had air raid shelters and every morning we had a rehearsal of how long it would take to get there. One morning there was a real air raid and we all had to leave our classrooms and go to the shelter. We heard the bomber coming over and drop three bombs. These landed two miles from the school, but only 200 yards from where I lived. My father saw the bombs leave the plane and he and my mother dashed into the house and hid under the table. A complete row of terraced houses was damaged and several people were killed that day.' (Dorothy Fowler – Ashton-on-Ribble WI)

▩ WAR EFFORT ▩

'We had an Anderson air raid shelter during the war, the type that was buried in the garden. My mother, who was an air raid warden, made my sister and me sleep in the shelter for the duration of the war. Initially we had hammocks but soon realised our mistake (we didn't make allowance for the sagging). After that it was bunks.

We lived in south Manchester, which was in the line of fire for Trafford Park. I worked in the Park and one day after various detours (which happened every day due to bomb damage) I arrived to find a massive hole where a four-storey building had stood. It had suffered a direct hit from a landmine. The staff were all found employment within the other factories and offices owned by the CWS.

My contribution to the war effort was to cut and prepare sandwiches through each Saturday night. We would then set off in mobile canteens at about 4 to 5 am and distribute refreshments to the men who were fire watching on most large buildings. They were mainly watching for incendiary bombs as these would cause a lot of damage but if caught in time could be dealt with satisfactorily with stirrup pumps and sand.' *(Edith Ryan – Little Lever WI)*

LIFE GOES ON

Whatever was happening around us, life had to go on and we soon learned to live with rationing and the blackout, and to accept the presence of soldiers and prisoners of war.

▣ THE FIRST DAY ▣

'The 3rd of September, 1939, a beautiful sunny hot day. Why do I remember it so clearly? It was the first day of the war.

I and three friends had been sharing two pairs of roller skates – we had one skate each. After playing for a couple of hours we sat down on the pavement, leaning against the house wall. Suddenly there was an almighty racket and we looked at each other in alarm. Mums and Dads appeared in doorways shouting to their children to come indoors *immediately*. I shot across the street – still with a skate on – into the house and under the stairs with Mum and Dad. When I say that Mum weighed a good 16 stone you can imagine it was quite a crush!

After about ten minutes Dad said, "Blow this, I'm hungry, get out and let's get on with the meal. If we stay here much longer we'll suffocate, never mind being bombed." That was the one and only time we went to shelter when the siren went.' (*Kath Cookson – Ulnes Walton WI*)

◼ WARTIME PRESTON ◼

'Our house overlooked Blackpool Road, known locally as "The New Road". When my mother was young it was a very minor road, surrounded by fields where gypsies sometimes camped. During the war, almost every week British and American Army convoys would drive along the road. If they were Americans we ran alongside shouting, "Any gum, chum?" and they would throw us gum and chocolate bars.

One day Winston Churchill was driven along the road. We all went to see him. He stood in a jeep, giving the Victory sign, a cigar in his mouth, looking exactly as he had on the news at the pictures. Another day the Queen, Princess Elizabeth and Princess Margaret came to visit Preston. We were allowed out of school to see them and everyone stood at the side of the road, waving the flags we had made in class.

My father drove a petrol tanker for Esso, but during the war the petrol companies merged and all the tankers were painted grey. He was also in the Home Guard and I can picture him now, sitting in the living room cleaning his rifle.

I remember shopping with my mother and queuing for food. One day she cooked us a lovely meal, which we thought was steak. She watched us eat it and then confessed it was horsemeat. You should have seen our faces!' (*Marion Sumner – Lea WI*)

'Our family lived at a public house in Preston, called the Moor Hall Inn (it has since been demolished and houses built on the site). It was a very close community, with regulars coming in each evening for their pint and a game of darts, and on Friday and Saturday nights for a good old sing-song, with the same people getting up to sing their favourite song. My aunt played the piano, and the applause for their songs was deafening.

Blackout restrictions were Dad's first priority, and what a job that was, making sure no cracks of light shone as customers came and went through the pub door. Dad propped up the cellar door, so that we could go down for safety if the sirens went. We had a heater of sorts down there, and some games and books to keep me and my sister Betty amused, in case we were down there for a long period of time. The sound of the air raid sirens scared me. I remember vividly when the first practice siren went. My sister was getting an ice cream from the "Stop me and buy one" bicycle which came round every day. She ran into the house crying, leaving her ice cream on the bicycle and a bemused vendor.

As I grew up and into my teens, the blackout held no fear for me when going out at night. Friends and I would go into town to dances or the pictures and walk home, perhaps calling for fish and chips on the way. We used to get some American soldiers and their girlfriends coming into the pub (always good spenders, as Dad used to say), and they often gave me and my sister chewing gum.

When peace was declared there was great rejoicing. Dad hung Union Jacks from each of our bedroom windows and so many reunions and celebrations took place as one by one the sons of families returned home. There always seemed to be a reason for a party in the pub, with singing and merrymaking and lots of happy faces. But we never forgot that there were young men who didn't return, causing such sadness for their families and friends.' *(Marie Mohan – Lea WI)*

▣ FEEDING THE ARMY ▣

'During the war years we coped with rationing, the blackout and all the restrictions that were imposed on us. The war often brought out the best in people: we helped each other, pooled our coupons if anyone got married and saved our dried fruit rationing for the wedding cake.

One night the Army arrived in Appley Bridge on manoeuvres and enquiries were made if there was a cafe in the village as they had not eaten all day. There wasn't, and we didn't have a cooker, just a Yorkshire range, but we managed to feed them all – a plate

Little James and his friend Fritz, prisoner of war, at Docker. Note the 'PW' initials on the knees of his trousers. (Emily Hacking – Leck & Cowan Bridge WI)

of chips, a slice of bread and a mug of tea each. Everyone in the lane helped with a few potatoes, a packet of margarine or a few slices of bread, making it a great team effort – and we fed the British Army! *(Joyce Walker – Appley Bridge WI)*

◈ PRISONERS OF WAR ◈

'Four German prisoners of war were sent to our farm at Docker. One helped my uncle on the farm and the other three worked with Dad harvesting farmers' crops in the summer and logging in the winter months. They were treated as part of the family, even singing duets at chapel. Many an evening was spent round the fire having a good old sing-song with them. Back in Germany one had been a blacksmith and another a butcher. My Dad's three were called Arnold, Fritz and Karl.

Arnold took a threshing outfit round the surrounding area on his own when crops were ready; he also did the book-keeping and collected the money. Fritz loved playing with us children, but when my small brother started speaking German before he could speak English, Karl had to stop! I can remember the tears that were shed the day they left us. My mother blamed it on the onions she was peeling.' *(Emily Hacking – Leck & Cowan Bridge WI)*

◈ A PRODIGAL ATTITUDE ◈

'Only six when the war started, my most vivid memory is of rationing. Mam had a very prodigal attitude, and when our grocery order was delivered on Friday she used it as if it was Christmas. When it had gone we did without – or used substitutes, such as saccharin for sugar. Our disapproving relatives never let us near their sugar bowls.

Dad, having bravely served in the Great War, was the only person who challenged this policy. Unfortunately, he suffered from a serious ailment – chronic hypochondria – and as he waited to see the doctor he would always chat to other people in the waiting room, who would give him their recipes to eke out the ration of, for instance, margarine. He would put these into

action while Mam was out working. The results were awful –
nasty pale, sloppy messes. We gave them a miss and reached out
for the dripping! As you may imagine, strong words passed and
but for the fact that he grew vegetables and kept hens, I think he
would have become another casualty of the war.

In later life Mam was advised to give up sugar for her health,
but she refused point-blank, saying that she had had enough
Hitlers during her lifetime.' *(Gladys Gawthorpe – Hapton WI)*

◈ A FARMER'S LAMENT ◈

'In 1941, under the Ministry's Lease-Lend Regulations, local
county "War-Ag" committees had to support every request for a
tractor and a questionnaire had to be filled out by the farmer.
This extra bureaucracy was a great irritant to hard working
farmers. One of the questions was: "State your reasons for
requiring this tractor". This provoked my father into writing *A
Farmer's Lament: a Lancashire Man's Despair at Lease-Lend Form-
Filling Regulations*, which gained some publicity.

"Don't think I want a tractor, lads, to take away my brass,
I want to grow some 'taters, corn and tons of grass,
It's no use keeping grousing when Owd Hitler's on yer track.
You ought to give us tractors fixed wi' guns and t'likes of that,
With a searchlight on the bonnet, and a tank to put at t'back.
With lots o' tanks and 'taters we could drive the blighter back.
If Jerry lands at Longton and I get to feeling queer,
I'll step on mi' tractor and I'm right for anyweer.
Please let me have a tractor, I'll see it works all right,
I can plough with it till bedtime, then be sowing corn all night,
Drive it home next morning, right up to the door,
Down a bit for breakfast, then go back and plough some more.
When this war is over and Hitler is no more,
You can have it back for eighteen pence, it won't be worth much
more.
When this job gets finished, there won't half be a do,
'Cos we can get our corn and 'taters from the lands of Timbuctoo.'
(Mona Lewis – Hoole WI)

The Hurst Green ladies' football team in 1944. (Jan Hardy – Hurst Green WI)

◈ FOOTBALL LADIES ◈

'In 1944 here in Hurst Green, the football stars were all ladies. During the war we played football regularly, coached by one of the few men remaining in Hurst Green – a former star forward of the all-male team. His training schedule made no concessions to the fact that we were women, or that we worked long hours at the bobbin mill doing the "men's work" and still had all the "women's work" to do at home.

A charity match for Salute the Soldier Week was held in Hurst Green on Saturday, 13th May, against the ladies of Clitheroe Town. A fortnight earlier we had beaten Clitheroe 4–1 and the Town team were wanting their revenge. The *Clitheroe Advertiser and Times* summed up the "brilliant dribbles, flashing shots, sensational saves, all served up by a bevy of comely girls – such was the football fare offered at Hurst Green last Saturday, where, for the first time in immediate local history, a match was played by ladies." We reached half time with the score 3–0 in our favour.

"urged on by a veritable Hampden roar from the home crowd, which made it clear that nothing short of complete annihilation of the visitors would satisfy them, the brilliant football of the village girls brought them five more goals."

It's funny how memory is both so vivid and yet so unreliable. I know that I sustained an injury during the match, that it was a tough one and that I scored three goals. However, the newspaper report says that Clitheroe played with ten "men" in the second half – funny, I felt sure we dispatched *three* of their players!' *(Jan Hardy – Hurst Green WI)*

▣ ON THE RADIO ▣

'At breakfast time during the war my family would sit round the table listening eagerly to the news. We heard reports of raids over London, news of our troops, statistics of our fighters lost over France, and took seriously all the hints and precautions given to us for making life a little easier and safer. My mother kept a pencil and paper handy on which she took down recipes and handy household tips. She became a wonder at a variety of dishes using dried eggs and corned beef.

We also listened to the advice of the Radio Doctor. He had a very comforting voice and gave little homilies on "taking care of one's chest" or the necessity to "keep regular habits".

At five o'clock I listened to *Children's Hour* with Uncle Mac, Auntie Muriel and Auntie Doris. Then after the washing up was done in the evening we gathered round the radio to listen to favourite programmes such as *Monday Night At Eight*, *The Happidrome*, *Much Binding in the Marsh*, or *ITMA*. Most households had just one set which took pride of place in the living room, and we sat round quietly, intently listening. There were only two channels, the Home Service and the Light Programme. Radio in those days was never just a noise in the background.' *(Marjorie Acton – Clayton-le-Woods WI)*

THE WOMEN'S LAND ARMY

With many farm workers called up into the Forces, the essential task of feeding Britain fell largely upon the shoulders of the Women's Land Army.

◈ JUST TURNED 17 ◈

'I was just turned 17 when the war began, living in a suburb of Liverpool with my mother, older brother and younger brother and sister. My father had died the previous year and we were all still trying to come to terms with that.

My younger brother and sister were evacuated but did not settle in their new surroundings and I was working in a bank in the city and not enjoying it, so when two of my friends from school decided to join the Land Army because they were very fond of animals, I persuaded my mother to let me join them.

We were sent to Hutton, the Lancashire Agricultural College, for two months' training, which we sadly needed, and arrived there early in March 1940. We were issued with corduroy breeches, two coffee-coloured aertex shirts, a green pullover, two pairs of dungarees, three pairs of khaki knee socks, a pair of heavy brown shoes, and a khaki-coloured felt brimmed hat. My friends, who had done some riding, were very critical of the cut of the breeches, but I was quite happy with my new outfit.

We had to be up early in the morning, while it was still dark, and at first only got to wash the cows' udders and clean out the shippons, but after we were more used to being at close quarters with the cows we learned to put on the milking machines and "strip" the cows of the last drops of milk by hand, something which is never done now, I think.

At first we did not want the huge breakfasts that were served, but after a week or two we were coming back for a second bowl of porridge, and buying packets of cream crackers and soft cheese which we ate in our rooms after the very good meals we

Muriel, with Fanny the horse who had a mind of her own. (Muriel Harrison – Bolton-le-Sands WI)

were given. There were girls from all walks of life; I remember one, Winnie, who had been a kitchen maid in a Liverpool restaurant. She was very pale and I thought quite sickly looking when she arrived, but it was amazing how she blossomed and became rounded and rosy cheeked.

After six weeks I was told that I was to be sent to a local farmer at Clifton, near Blackpool, and I arrived there somewhat apprehensively, as I had of course left behind my two friends. The farm was run by Mr Tomlinson and his sister, overseen by their elderly mother. They were very kind to me, pitied my ignorance of country ways and taught me with wonderful patience. I had never learned to ride a bike as in Liverpool one had only to jump on a tram and could go anywhere in the city for twopence, but the country was different and my new boss taught me to ride the farm bike which everyone seemed to use, although it had hardly any brakes. Soon I was quite confident on it. I had only been able to ride it a few days when he sent me to the smithy with a horse's collar over my shoulder to be repaired. If I expressed any doubt of my ability he used to say, "Never let it be said your mother bred a jibber!"

I worked there several months, but in the autumn Mr Tomlinson went to Ulverston where they still held hiring fairs, really to hire a farm maid, but he came back having also found a strapping farm lad whom he had hired for the following year. The people looking for work used to go to the fair wearing emblems to show their trade, and were hired by the year, the bargain being closed by slapping hands and, I think, payment of a shilling.

I was then sent to a large poultry farm near Carnforth, on Warton Crag. I was greeted by the farmer, Mr Harrison, and his wife and made to feel welcome, then met their second son, Ken, who just a year older than me.

Ken and I did most of the poultry farming, and it was hard work. Every afternoon we spent quite a long time cleaning and packing eggs. Mr Harrison mostly looked after the cows and reared the calves. Ken had a motorbike of which he was very proud and I was soon riding on the back of it, going up into the Lake District or to the pictures in Carnforth. The Carnforth picture house changed its programme three times a week and often we went at least twice. This, when Ken's mother used to put our wages, one pound for me and ten shillings for Ken, on the sideboard every Saturday. Fortunately Ken was a very good shot and made enough money from rabbits and the occasional pheasant to pay for running his motorbike and trips to the pictures, even going in the expensive seats, upstairs at one shilling and ninepence. If we were really wealthy we would have an evening at the Winter Gardens, Morecambe, where there were still some excellent shows.

With poultry stocks decreasing there was less and less work for me and I was spending most of my time scraping empty hen cabins until they were spotlessly clean, a somewhat boring job which I did not feel was helping the war effort very much, so after discussion with Mr Harrison, I applied for another transfer.

I was sent to a farm in the cotton town of Darwen, or rather just outside it. When I arrived I found that the farmer, Mr Kershaw, had asked for a girl who could milk. Well, I could milk, but not without the help of a milking machine. However, he told me that he and his wife liked the look of me, so if I would work hard at learning to milk they would keep me! It was hard work, and my arms and fingers ached as I tried to match Mr Kershaw's skill. He gave me the drying-off cows to practise on and no doubt I hastened the process of their drying-off, but gradually I became more proficient although I was never as skilled as the farmer was.

The milk was loaded, in two churns, into a milk float, a kind of two-wheeled trap, pulled by a horse called Fanny, who was very beautiful but had a somewhat uncertain temper. She loved to take a bite at me, particularly when I was tightening her girth, when she would blow herself out so that the strap was loose when she relaxed. I had to learn the milk round, first in the "posh area" of Darwen and then down among the millhouses. At first Fanny knew the round better than I did, and if she stopped and there was a jug of milk on a doorstep I filled it. I had a pint and a half pint measure inside the churn and customers mostly left a jug with a saucer on top on their doorstep. I had two crates of milk for the fussy customers who preferred their milk in a bottle.

Milk, like most most things, was rationed to three pints per person per week. This meant that where there were only two people in a house they were supposed to have a milkless day, and single people, mostly old ladies on their own, only got half a pint six days a week. However, there were a few large families who did not take their full ration and so I was usually able to let my old ladies have their extra half pint.

Fanny was a most precocious horse. She did not like women in fur coats, and if she saw one she would try to mount the pavement and snap at her. Also, she did not like tramcars, and if she heard one coming up behind her she would take off and race along the street, turning corners with the milk float on one wheel. Two of my lady customers used to wait at their gates with a crust for Fanny and I could not get her to wait for me to deliver the milk to the houses before these. Usually I came out to find Fanny had already gone on ahead and was enjoying her snack. At the end of the round, on a Friday, I would call in at the grocery shop to pick up the week's order and once, having spent more time than I should chatting to the shopkeeper, I came out to find no trace of Fanny. The groceries were heavy and I was very glad when another farmer came by and gave me a lift home. When I got there Fanny was in her stable, unharnessed and enjoying her hay.

Sometimes we had casual workers, vagrants really, who stayed a few days, worked for their keep and slept in the barn or the passage in the cowshed. One of the younger ones was a deserter from the Merchant Navy. When Mr Kershaw asked him why he had deserted he replied, "Bluddy job war'nt safe, Harry, bluddy job war'nt safe." He was with us for Christmas and on Christmas Day Mr Kershaw and he volunteered to do the milk round. They had strict instructions not to dawdle as Christmas dinner would be waiting. However, it was three o'clock before they arrived back, having been celebrating Christmas very thoroughly with the customers on the round. As the horse and float came into view Mrs Kershaw said with some surprise that they must be all right as Harry was standing up in the float, but as it drew nearer it became obvious that he was being supported on one side by Jim, and on the other side by his nephew. Both men went straight to bed, one upstairs and the other in the cowshed. When they had recovered Mr Kershaw said that the moment he put his head on the pillow the room started spinning round. "Eh," said Jim, "tha shoulda bin int' shippon, there war a bluddy stampede."

My mother had taken my younger brother and sister to Australia, where she had two brothers, to get away from the bombing, and my elder brother was in London, so I applied for yet another transfer to be nearer to him. Also, I must admit, things were very quiet in my part of Lancashire, although poor Liverpool was taking a hammering from the bombs, and I actually felt I wanted to be a little more involved in this war we were fighting, and so I was transferred to Kent, where I worked on farms until the end of the war, when Ken came back from the Far East and we were married ten days later, as we still are, 50 years years on.' *(Muriel Harrison – Bolton-le-Sands WI)*

❖ VERY HARD WORK ❖

'When I was first informed that I had to join the Women's Land Army I was filled with absolute horror! Having never been keen to help in the garden and straight from four years of office work, I was a very raw recruit.

My first impression in Scarisbrick was of the vast areas of crops and weeds! Go down with the other three land girls I was told, to hand-weed the caulies. The weeds came up to my waist. We did this over a three week period – so what now, we asked? We had hoped for something different, feeling proud to have finished the last job, only to be told to start again at the other end of the field!

There were days of cutting cabbage, but of course the girls were not allowed to use the knives – we had to hold and hump up and down the hundredweight bags. Cabbages for the forces! Days were spent doing the same with cauliflowers, but they were loaded, instead of bagged, onto trailers and stacked neatly; amazing how they never fell off. Endless days of picking sprouts, sometimes so hard with the frost we could have done with a hammer to break them off the stalks. The hours between 3 pm and 5 pm were the worst and longest. If we kept picking, the day went quicker and we were warmish, but if we stopped just to look at them and have a moan then our hands would become unbearable. No breaks in those days with a hot flask of coffee.

In the early days the corn was cut by hand around the outside edges of the field, then with a machine which turned out sheaves. These had to be stood upright, six or eight at a time, so they could dry in the sun. If it rained we would have to spread them around, then restack before evening, so we had scratchy arms which were sore already with the sun!

Potato planting was a back-breaking job, especially for us girls, but there was no mention of aching backs or legs to the men, we would not be called "soft". Cabbage planting, before the machine arrived to make life easier, was another back-breaker. Sometimes we had 14 planters across the field – all male of course, we womenfolk had to hand out the bunches of plants (not too many) from the heavy boxes we carried. If the plants were large, there was the everlasting cry of "plants" from the men, who delighted in doing this. Sometimes to avoid wasting valuable land there were cabbages planted in between the potato crop so we had to step over these when putting in the potatoes, not good for the legs or back!

The Irishmen came over for the digging of potatoes and lived in the "shant" on the farm, about four or six in number; they were usually friends and from southern Ireland. It was our job (one girl at a time) to weigh and stitch up the sacks. We had to carry a heavy frame made of thick wood and a heavy weighing clock up and down the field. As they reached the end of the field they would walk back to start again. The best time for me was when I had a jeep – left-hand drive (American variety), and that was a lot of fun carrying this heavy equipment up and down the field. I used to give the men a lift up to the farm at lunch time – they were grateful but always glad to get off!

Over the years we had German and Italian prisoners of war to help us. They came from all walks of life, so some were useless and unwilling, while others pleasant enough and very helpful. They used to boil loads of potatoes to eat with their lunch. They went back in the evening in trucks with guards to their camp.

Hoeing was a popular job as we were able to chat while working. Carrots, beetroot and small plants were weeded on our knees, "scrawling" it was called, when we tied clean sacks around our knees and crawled along the drills. This was usually an evening job on piecework and if the ground was soft (on the moss, for instance) we could "make quite a nice sum". Sounds hard, but we actually all enjoyed it.' *(Mrs G. Haughton – c/o Aughton Moss WI)*

◈ THE BOYS LIKED US ◈

'I lived at Bury and at 17 years of age in 1943 I had never been away from home, so I decided to be a land girl. My first posting was at Blackburn and I felt as if I was going to the end of the earth. My father decided he would go with me to make sure the couple I was billeted with were all right (not that he could do anything about it). As it happens they were super. I worked for the War Agriculture and Fisheries. All winter I helped on the threshing machine going to different farms. One particular time I was driving the tractor in Blackburn when I got the front iron wheels in the tram lines and had to go to the end of the line to get them out!

Summer came and the boss decided I should stay in the office and clean machinery. I was pretty bored so I took my knitting. When I saw the boss coming I started cleaning the machinery. Eventually he said, "For goodness sake girl, stop cleaning and bring your knitting."

I was missing all the lovely weather so I complained to the Land Army who said land girls had not to do office work. I was then sent to Pilling. I arrived at four o'clock only to find a brand new bicycle waiting for me and was told I had to ride to Cockerham the following day. As I had never been on a bike in my life you can imagine the horror I felt, so I had to learn pretty quickly that night.

I lived in a hostel (just wooden huts) behind Pilling church with 16 girls and a warden who ruled us with a rod of iron. We had to be in by ten o'clock at night and got one late pass a month until twelve so we could go to a dance. Even then we had to

Land girls from Pilling Hostel – it wasn't all hard work! (Marjorie Lund – Whitechapel & Inglewhite WI)

knock on her door to report.

On Cockerham Moss I worked with two more girls and eight men. My first job was sorting potatoes and being a towny I had never heard of seed potatoes, so there I was taking all the shoots off until a very nice foreman stopped me.

We had a lovely time at the hostel. All the girls got on well – I can't remember even a wrong word being spoken. We organised dances and concerts and I must say we had some very talented girls, apart from me. I used to draw the curtains and see to the props.

We were allowed to go home once a month, Friday night until Sunday night, and there was one week's leave every six months. It took quite a long time to get home; a bus from Pilling to Garstang, then to Preston, then to Bolton and finally to Bury. One time I missed the last bus to Pilling due to fog so I had to walk. I arrived with holes in my stockings and blisters.

We finished the work we had to do on Cockerham Moss, so we

A land girl's wedding at Pilling – how could one standard issue hat achieve so many shapes and angles? (Marjorie Lund – Whitechapel and Inglewhite WI)

started working for Mr Houghton at Pilling. It was a mixed farm with cows, hens and market gardening. Our first day he told us to milk the cows. We had only seen cows in a field so how could we milk them? He was very nice with us and it didn't take us long to learn. I had some of the happiest days of my life there. We worked with two men and even though it seemed as if we got all the rough work like digging the paddocks with a spade and spreading manure with a fork from heaps in the field, we really did enjoy the work, even hoeing fields of lettuce all day.

Then came a very sad day when we were told the hostel was closing and we were all being sent to different places away from Pilling. Lots of tears were shed that day as I was courting my future husband and many of the other girls had Pilling boys. I was one of the lucky ones as Mr Houghton didn't want to lose us so he managed to get us billets with a very nice couple who had one son. There was just one problem, they did not have a bathroom, just a tin bath hung up in the yard so when we wanted a bath we had to make sure the husband and son were out for the night.

We lived there quite a long time until they decided it was too much for them, so we moved to a new place. Funnily enough, I can't remember them having a bath at all! We just had to have a good wash and wait until we went home to have a bath. They had a pet hen named Gertie. One day she went missing and after three days they found her. She had fallen into the earth closet lavatory! The couple decided to give us a treat, we would have Gertie for dinner the following day. You can imagine what our thoughts were. All we could think about was what the hen had been living on for the past three days. Well, it was wartime so we just had to grin and bear it and pretend we enjoyed it.

Even though it was hard work I really enjoyed my time in the Land Army – though the Pilling girls didn't seem to like us, the boys did. Out of 16 girls five of us married local boys.' (*Marjorie Lund – Whitechapel and Inglewhite WI*)

A CHILD'S WAR

The dangers and insecurities of wartime meant that children had to grow up fast – particularly those who were evacuated far from homes and families.

▣ SOMETHING WAS HAPPENING TO MY WORLD ▣

'In the summer of 1939 I was 13 years old. Wars and rumours of wars were not uppermost in my mind, more important were plans for the lovely long seven weeks summer holiday. My friends and I spent our time playing tennis, lying on the beach and swimming in the sea.

Towards the end of August I think I realised that all the jokes about Hitler were becoming serious, and that newspapers were predicting war with Germany. Something was happening to my safe, happy world.

My father left his job and went to visit his mother and sister in Bolton. This during the week was very unusual, visiting was always weekends, when my family went together. On Friday, 1st September my father left by train for Preston to report to Fulwood Barracks, as he was in the Army Reserve. Before he went he hugged us all, assured my mother, "It will soon be over", and told my sister and me to be good girls.

Sunday, 3rd September and at 11 am everyone was listening to the radio to hear Neville Chamberlain announce that we were at war with Germany. But it still seemed a long way away. Foreign holidays then were for the wealthy and going to London was an adventure.

Our house was quite large, so my mother had promised the billeting officer that she would take four evacuees. Blackpool was considered a safe area. Four little girls about eight or nine years old duly arrived, but I remember one poor mum accompanied by eight or ten children trailing round trying to find beds. My mother felt so sorry for them that she took them in as well until the next day, when other arrangements could be made. It was chaos but at least they were all fed, washed and put to bed, some three in a bed. I thought it was wonderful.

The four little girls stayed, visited by tearful mothers every couple of weeks, but were taken home to Manchester just before Christmas, as everything seemed so quiet.

We had gone back to school, but had to share with a convent school from near Manchester. For two weeks we went to school from 8 am until noon, then we met at the church hall in the afternoon from 1 pm until 3 pm. When it was fine we went on nature walks, or if it was wet we knitted or read in the hall. The other school had 10 am to noon at the hall, then school from 1 pm to 5 pm. Then we changed over for two weeks. Contractors came in and built air raid shelters on the school playing fields, and we had air raid drill. Everyone had a gas mask in a little square cardboard box, which we all quickly found covers for. But they were a nuisance to carry, as we had a satchel full of books as well. We didn't mind the air raid drill at first, as we missed a few lessons, but it soon became a bit tedious.

In Blackpool, by this time, there were a lot of Air Force personnel doing their training and a lot of foreign troops. Some of these were Polish and it was interesting to hear them sing as they marched along to training classes.

By this time I think we had ration books, but I can only remember a shortage of bananas and oranges. People seemed to join queues for anything whether they needed it or not. Also it had its social aspect, as people chatted to one another as they waited. Shopkeepers were very fair as a rule, but if you were a good customer there was often something "under the counter". *(Joyce Smith – Clayton-le-Woods WI)*

❖ PRACTICE INTO REALITY ❖

'In August 1939 I was a 15 year old schoolgirl attending Stretford High School for Girls. It was decided that a practice evacuation of schoolchildren should take place. My parents agreed that my sister and I should take part in this scheme and we were eventually put on a train at Old Trafford with the other girls. When we arrived at our destination – Macclesfield – we were met by a host of officials who sorted us into age groups and took us to the homes (billets) we were to share. My sister and I were split up but billeted near to each other. I shared a lovely big modern house with my schoolfriend. The lady of the house was rather taken aback when we arrived on her doorstep as she was expecting two small children and had not bargained for two teenagers who could eat her out of house and home. However, we all enjoyed our stay. We shared Macclesfield High School using it alternate weeks, and when not at the school we had our lessons in a church hall. Sadly, this practice evacuation became a reality when war was declared in September and I stayed at Macclesfield until I left school the following summer and returned home to Old Trafford.' *(Mary Pickthall – Hoghton WI)*

❖ HAPPY DAYS ❖

'I was eleven years old when war was declared and at that time lived in Barrow in Furness – then in Lancashire. The vicar of St George's church – Mr Beddows – gave me my gas mask and made sure it fitted properly. The WRVS were collecting anything aluminium and distributing clothes and blankets sent from

America. I was lucky in so much as I had a cousin in British Columbia who was the same age and fortunately for me the same size and she kept me looking quite smart during the period of clothes coupons.

Barrow organised a Spitfire fund to do their bit for the war effort, and I can remember my mother embroidering a tablecloth to raffle. It was a tremendous effort, but between raffles and donations eventually they met the target.

The bombing became very fierce and Barrow really got a pasting. My father took my mother, grandmother and me to the top of the hill just outside Dalton in Furness where we could look across and see the fires burning as the bombs dropped on Barrow. I don't think I will ever forget my father saying, "That's our house," and next morning after being in the car all night we went back and sure enough both our house and my Gran's house were devastated. I can't imagine what he must have felt when he saw the mess as he had built it.

After this we went to live on a farm and there began one of the happiest times of my life. A very different way of life whichever way you look are it. The first thing that comes to my mind is Bess, the lovely carthorse that used to be yoked to the milk float, and I went with the farmer to deliver the milk out of the big milk churns with the pint and gill measures. Bess would also be yoked up to the plough and the farmer would guide her in straight lines down the field with me tagging on behind.

Leisure time was taken up playing cards – mainly Newmarket and whist, or knitting socks for the troops. There was an occasional dance in the village hall and when I was quite a bit older I was allowed to go. I can remember doing the Lancers and getting bruised arms in the process!

Schooldays were severely interrupted. The boys' and girls' schools were next to each other, and our headmistress called a few girls at a time into her study to teach us the facts of life. A photograph of a male was shown to each one of us in turn and passed on to the next girl with great rapidity, so we weren't very much wiser when we came out of the study than when we went in!' *(Joyce Simm – Crag Bank WI)*

The Whit Walk Queen at Pendleton in 1939. Many children were disappointed when the war meant the Walks were cancelled 'for the duration'. (Joyce Ball – Little Lever WI)

▨ WE WOULD DIE TOGETHER ▨

'I was nine years old when war broke out and I attended Halton Bank school in Pendleton, Salford. We were to be evacuated to Ulverston and we were all lined up at the bus stop with our gas masks in little brown cardboard boxes and our name labels pinned to our coats when my mother decided if we had to die we would all die together. So I was taken from the line and never got to Ulverston.

I also attended St Thomas's church and Sunday school in Pendleton. We always had our Whit Walks on Whit Friday afternoon when we walked down Broad Street to Leaf Square where we had milk and biscuits before walking back again. In 1938 and 1939 I was a train bearer to the Sunday school Queen and was picked to be Queen in 1940, but the walks were cancelled and they didn't resume until after the war was over so I missed out on being Queen.

In 1939 we lived in Sutton flats. There were 24 flats on four floors in each block. Each block had its own concrete and brick shelter in a clearing next to the block of flats. I remember that we had two small attache cases permanently packed. One had the policies and private papers in it and the other had a clean change of underwear in case of emergencies. As the sirens went we had to get into our siren suits which my mam had made out of old coats for my brother and me and I had to make sure that I carried one of the cases. Mam took the other one as well as carrying my brother, who was three at the time. In the shelter we had bunk beds and camp beds. It was cold and damp in the winter so we had a paraffin stove to keep us warm. We had a wind-up gramophone and games to keep us entertained.

We had some good times and some scary times, especially when a landmine dropped on a bank nearby. That night my Dad was on duty as a Home Guard sergeant. He came home with a piece of the mine as a souvenir.

I did my bit for the war effort. I used to help out with the blackout blinds at the school as my grandfather was caretaker there.' (*Joyce Ball – Little Lever WI*)

▨ GROWING UP SO FAST ▨

'The day before my seventh birthday was hot. I came out of school early and tar bubbled between the cobbles and the tramlines glistened in the sun as I dawdled down the hill. My bag felt heavy. In it I had a nightdress, towel and toothbrush. I passed the street where the weaving shed was. My mother was in there, working, and I wanted to go and get a hug but wasn't allowed in. My father was on "war work", so I had to go on alone. I crossed the town centre, walked uphill and soon arrived at my destination. I was very frightened. I knew I would not see my mother again for four days.

I pushed open the heavy door, shivered in the sudden coolness and walked to the desk. I was led through another huge door and down a corridor. The figure in blue checked my bag and said sternly, "You've forgotten your gas mask. You'll have to go back for it, be quick, we can't admit you after four o'clock."

The following day they took out my tonsils. We had to grow up so fast in those days.' (*Pat Keightley – Hapton WI*)

'I was born in the cotton town of Darwen. It is a small town surrounded on all sides by hills. There are very few streets or roads that are not built on slopes or "brews" and our house was at the top of several.

We were a small family – mother, father and me – and even smaller when my father went to war. I was only five when he went away and I became used to his absences. It seemed quite normal to me, as to many of my friends, that our fathers only came home "on leave". However, when I was eight he was sent abroad to the Far East and it was well over two years before I saw him again.

After he had gone my mother seemed very sad. I didn't realise my father's danger, but it worried me to see her like this. Also she looked pale and often felt sick, but she still had to go to work. Money was always in short supply.

In those days my mother was everything to me. She was the centre of my small world. I had accepted my life without my father, but I couldn't imagine what I would do without her. She was not a robust person, even though she was clever and energetic. Sometimes she took jobs that were too physically demanding for her, but at this time she had what I thought was a nice job. She was manageress of a dress shop in the town.

On this particular winter evening it was very dark. Of course, there were never any street or house lights, because of the blackout, but that night it was overcast, even threatening snow. We could not close the shop until 7 pm, even though we had no customers for hours. however, at last the doors were locked, but we could not go home until the electricity was turned off. As usual, Mother had to go down into the cellar to do this. The cellar was entered from some steps in the yard at the back. Mother and Stella, one of her young assistants, went out and we stood in the doorway ready to go. Unfortunately Stella dropped the torch which was guiding Mother, just as she reached the top of the cellar steps. In the darkness Mother slipped and fell straight down, some ten or twelve feet.

I remember screaming, "Mummy, Mummy," but there was no reply. I thought she was dead and even Mrs Waddicor, the lady who did the alterations, seemed very worried. However, at last the torch was found and the girls rushed down. Eventually, thankfully Mother revived and seemed all right, at least she said she was. It was impossible to see in the dark.

We had missed the bus, they only came every two hours, and had to walk home, up several of the "brews". I chattered on, telling Mother how frightened I had been and how glad I was that she was not hurt, but she didn't answer. We walked more and more slowly and I began to realise that she was ill. To make matters worse it began to snow.

At last we reached home and I could see that Mother was very ill, but she insisted on lighting the fire. She told me to get the big pile of newspapers we were saving for the war effort. Some she used for the fire, but the others, strangely, she piled on the chair and then sat down. I was very frightened.

Minutes went by. I could see something was terribly wrong. Then I notice the chair and the newspapers – slowly, but surely, they were turning red. Mother was bleeding. She began to sway backwards and forwards, groaning. I wanted to scream, but all I did was sit, petrified. At last she roused herself. "Knock on the wall. Keep knocking until Mrs Bamber comes, then let her in."

I did as I was told and finally I heard Mrs Bamber's answering knock and rushed to open the door. Mrs Bamber, like us, had a husband in the forces and she had a small baby, but thankfully she came. She made Mother a drink and I sat as they talked. They seemed to forget I was there. The word "miscarriage" was mentioned and "embarkation leave". Now I realise Mother must have become pregnant during my father's last leave before he went abroad, but then I had no idea what had happened, I just knew "miscarriage" was something very dreadful. Obviously the fall had caused it to happen.

Finally Mrs Bamber told me that she was going to get help and I must be very good and quiet because she might be a long time. How she managed I never found out. We lived quite out in the wilds and had no phone. What she did with her baby, or if she got someone else to get help I will never know, but I know whatever she did, took a very long time, a very long time indeed.

When she had gone Mother told me to go to bed, but I couldn't have left her. I sat and watched as the scarlet stain grew larger and Mother continued to rock backwards and forwards, groaning quietly to herself. After a while she seemed to go to sleep, but then woke with an even louder groan. I put coal on the fire and tried to cover her up, but for the most part I just sat, almost afraid to breathe in case it made the pain worse.

Hours went by. I went to the window and saw the snow sweeping by. I felt that if someone did not come soon she would surely die. Just when I felt that I could not stand another second, helplessly watching Mother rocking and groaning, I heard the lock turn and in came my grandmother and a tall lady, with a strange accent. She was the doctor – an Irish lady.

Immediately all was bustle. I was sent to bed, but not to sleep. I could hear voices and noise, but I was strangely comforted by the sounds, especially the Irish lilt when the doctor spoke. Finally the bedroom door opened and my grandmother entered.

"Don't worry anymore, your Mummy isn't going to die," she said. I fell asleep, lulled by her gentle snores, ending the longest and most terrible night of my short life.

Thankfully, Mother recovered, although it took a long time. My father came home and two years later my little sister was born, quite safely, so all ended happily; but although I don't remember bombs or shells very well and even rationing and shortages are only dim memories, I will never forget that night. It is as clear as yesterday.' *(Muriel Spencer – Bradshaw and Harwood WI)*

❖ EVACUATED TO LYTHAM ❖

'Sometimes when I see pictures and films of evacuees, I wonder why they all have suitcases and brown paper parcels. At my school in New Moston, Manchester we were only allowed to have a haversack, knapsack or a rucksack dependent on what your mother said!

I was eleven, my eldest brother and my youngest brother seven. And there were another four boys at home, one a baby and the other three all working and hoping to go into the forces. My father was a police inspector and was on duty for the three days before we were evacuated so we hadn't seen him, but we were more concerned with our new rucksacks.

We were taken by bus to the Victoria train station. We had labels pinned on us with names, where we were from and where we were going to. In our case it was Lytham, near Blackpool.

Our father was very strict with us, and me in particular, so I very seldom mentioned him to my friends. I was most surprised when one of my friends said there was a policeman heading our way. It was my father, in full uniform complete with Sam Browne belt. He warned us about being on our best behaviour and shook hands with each of us, even me his only daughter. He then presented us with a 7 lb tin of wine gums, "ration them out, they will last you for some weeks", and off he went, marshalling the school kids onto the train.

We all got on our train, opened the tin and within half an hour it was emptied. The tin was then thrown out of the window. Of course, everyone had a share, we had no chance of making them last.

Our mother had warned us about staying together; she told my brother Bob he was in charge and we were not to be split up. When we arrived in Lytham, we were left in a large hall. Suddenly our bravado was starting to leave us. Anybody could come to pick a child to take home. We clung to each other; some people asked me to go with them but they did not want the boys, other people wanted my younger brother but not us older ones. Bob put his arm around us and we all stayed together. We were the last children left in the hall and our teachers were beginning to despair. I expect they wanted to go to their digs too. Eventually the headmaster said to Bob, "We are splitting you up just for tonight, the boys are going with Mrs Fisher and Joyce is going with Mrs Salthouse."

As it happens, this family were very kind to me but I had to share a bed with their daughter of 19. I, being the only girl, had never shared a bed with anyone and neither had she! The toilet was at the end of the garden; this was another culture shock, we lived in a modern house with a bathroom and a separate wc. On Fridays they dragged a zinc bath off the wall outside and it was filled with kettles of hot water. I had to bath in front of the fire while the husband sat and read his newspaper. I didn't like that because I was always taught to be very private.

On the plus side, we went to school one week in the morning and one week in the afternoon. The locals changed to the time we weren't there. The local children hated us, they did all sorts of things to upset us and imitated our speech. (We thought they talked funny as well.) We were allowed into the pictures half price, the local kids tried it on but were soon found out.

After three months my mother wanted us back home. She said if we are going to be killed we may as well all be killed together.'
(Joyce McLellan – Staining WI)

▩ To Ashurst Beacon ▩

'Born in what was Lancashire but is now Merseyside, I was evacuated to a small cottage near Ashurst Beacon, south Lancashire. This was a two up, two down cottage, with a sink in the kitchen but the cold water came from a pump outside which serviced the row of houses. Two families lived here – my parents and I in the front bedroom – and shared the kitchen. There was no bathroom, and oddly enough I never remember going to the toilet – presumably it was a "privy" in the small yard cum neglected garden at the back. Our furniture was put in store in a pub's barn near the Beacon and there it stayed until we were offered "rooms" with the local chemist and his wife in the nearby village of Up Holland.

Schooldays were in the little village school. We used slates and chalk and with a small friend I walked to school morning and afternoon, with lunch at home. This was a distance of about half a mile, and we were not frightened of walking on our own then. The children laughed at my wellingtons because they were short, ankle-length ones. We sat out in the playground when the sun was hot and I remember wearing a rather old-fashioned sunbonnet.

There was little or no traffic on the road, but buses were more frequent, every quarter of an hour past our house. The mines were still very active and early in the morning lying in bed I could hear the miners in their clogs walking past our house to catch the very early buses which started (I think) about five or six o'clock in the morning from Abbey Lakes. As a schoolgirl later in

192

The boys and girls of the Lancaster concert party, with 'Auntie Lucy'
seated in the centre. (Dorothy Carter – Borwick and Priest Hutton WI)

Wigan I remember seeing them after the shifts had finished
covered top to toes in coal dust and down on their haunches on
the pavements waiting for buses to take them home. We tried to
avoid getting too close to them for our clothes would have been
black too!

The ending of the war was a special day as there was no
school, and after a trip to Liverpool, at home there was a bonfire
with potatoes roasted in it on the field behind our house. Later
we walked up to the ruined mill near the Beacon to get a view
over the Lancashire plain to the sea and to count the number of
bonfires we could see burning.' *(Audrey Laird – Aughton Moss WI)*

✦ Our Concert Party ✦

'During the last years of the war a small concert party was
initiated in Lancaster by Lucy Thomson, a millworker and
neighbour of my family. She gathered the local children together
to create a show to raise funds for a Lancaster bomber.

We rehearsed in a cellar a few doors away. Costumes were
produced by parents, our "music" was Auntie Lucy singing and

us joining in any bits we knew, and one or two of the members attended a local dancing class but mainly we were all "green". We produced tap dancing in the chorus line, some ballet items, and there was always a boy soprano soloist. My sister also sang solo numbers, and there were some monologues – really poetry recitals.

We performed in village halls all over the Lune Valley. Once we girls had to dress and change in the coal cellar, and climb over a heap of coke to reach the stage. There were usually pop bottle crates to climb on to reach the "stage", often very shaky constructions. But it was always worthwhile for the enthusiastic, crowded audiences. Eventually we had to disband the gang, but it was fun, and hard work, while it lasted.' *(Dorothy Carter – Borwick and Priest Hutton WI)*

▣ WAR AT PRIEST HUTTON ▣

'The school at Priest Hutton was in the building which was formerly the village tithe barn. It was extended in 1897, the year after the local church was built ann had been used for Sunday services before then. Unfortunately it closed in 1978 and is now a house.

I started at the school on 14th August 1939 and had just got settled in when the war began on 3rd September. On 1st September the evacuees arrived. There were 37 children and one teacher from Salford, and I can remember them standing outside the school looking lost whilst the billeting officer found homes for them. We were allocated a little girl about my age and the first thing she did was to sit in my doll's cot and go straight through the bottom. She did not stay with us long but went to live with an elderly couple who spoilt her. Soon after that we had a mother and baby to stay, but she was a city type and could not settle in the country. Soon after the evacuees arrived all the apple trees were stripped of their fruit as the children had not seen them growing before, only in shops.

When the school had to cope with these extra numbers, the sitting room of the school house, occupied by the caretaker, was taken over as an extra classroom and we infants were installed in there with our usual teacher. The evacuee teacher took care of the junior age range and the headmistress taught the senior children.

There were no modern facilities at the school and the toilets were of the primitive earth closet type. These were inspected from time to time by the Sanitary Inspector but they did not smell very nice. When I attended the school we had coal fires and oil lamps. Electricity for lighting was not installed until 1947 although school dinners had started in 1945 and an electric boiler was put in.

During the 1930s and 1940s there were quite a few outbreaks of infectious illness – diphtheria, measles, mumps and chickenpox, but I was very lucky and did not catch any of them. At one point the school had to be closed and fumigated and I can also remember a room at my Grandma's house being fumigated when her evacuee got scarlet fever.

During the war the children knitted comforts for the forces and parcels were sent off to minesweepers and others. All the boys at the school were taught to knit as well as the girls.

In May 1941 it was War Weapons Week. The school was closed for half a day and we all marched down to Borwick, about ¾ mile, and back again. There was an assembly on the village green outside the school and Lord and Lady Crawford spoke from a hay cart with chairs on it. The next year it was Warship Week and the year after, Wings for Victory Week. The children held school concerts in aid of these weeks.

I was brought up at the village shop, which was very much affected by the war and rationing. We were not allowed to sell things like butter or lard because we were only a small village and could not get enough registered customers. Instead we had to get our rations from the Co-op travelling shop, which stopped outside our shop. My grandma, who lived alone in the village, used to get very small portions. The butter and lard was cut off a big block and weighed out, and the sugar came in blue bags, also weighed from loose sugar. We did sell sweets and had to collect the coupons from people's ration books. They were very small and we had to count them and use them to buy more sweets from our supplier. When the sweets finally came off the ration, 1951 I think, we were sold out within an hour of opening because a party of young people who were staying locally got in before the locals. After that we used to keep some "under the counter" for the regular customers.

We had soldiers billeted near to us at Borwick and befriended quite a lot of them who were feeling lonely away from home for the first time and missing their families. My grandma and my mother used to provide accommodation for their wives so that they could come for a visit. We kept in touch with lots of them for years afterwards. At Christmas one year I got a small fairy cycle, but could not ride a two-wheeler. We had invited some of the soldiers for Christmas that year and by the end of the day they had taught me to ride the bike. The soldiers used our village Memorial Hall as a meeting place and set up a canteen there. Some of the rations from the canteen found their way to our house and my mother used to serve cups of tea from the kitchen window when they were out on manoeuvres. One of them kept a look-out for the sergeant and if he was seen they all disappeared down the lane, which was where they should have been in the first place.

We did not go short of food as we were registered as poultry keepers. We had to give up our egg ration but in return were allowed coupons to buy poultry meal. We used to mix this with potato peelings and other scraps, and it was cooked in an old pan, which made rather an unpleasant smell in the kitchen. We were able to eat the hens when they had stopped laying. Dad and I used to go into the hen-hut when it was dark and I had to shine a torch along the row of roosting hens for him to choose the one he wanted. It was impossible to catch them in daylight. We also kept ducks which were hatched out under a broody hen. We had a beck at the bottom of the garden, and the ducks were let out after ten o'clock as they were supposed to lay their eggs by then. They disappeared on to the beck for the rest of the day but always came home at dusk when they were locked up for the night. They also ended up on our plates. My uncle was in the Home Guard and he used rabbits for target practice, so we were able to eat them as well. We had a large garden so we were able to grow all kinds of vegetables, and Dad had a large greenhouse in which he grew tomatoes which we sold in the shop.

Lord Crawford speaking during War Weapons Week in May 1941 on Priest Hutton village green. In the background is the village school. (June Haythornthwaite – Borwick and Priest Hutton WI)

Dad was a guard on the railway and this was classed as a reserve occupation. He worked a lot of nights and had to go to places like Manchester and Barrow in Furness which were always being bombed. We used to go on day trips to places like Manchester and Liverpool; I used to enjoy Liverpool as they had trams and the overhead railway. In Manchester we visited the parents of one of the soldiers who had a butcher's shop. We came back with a huge parcel of lard and my mother kept worrying about it on the rack of the train. When we got it home she kept it covered up with a tea towel in the pantry. She was able to make pies for ages as we had plenty of fruit.

When Dad was working at night my mother and I often used to sleep at Grandma's house. One night while we were there a German plane, on its way back from Barrow, emptied its bombs nearby, just missing both the railway and the main A6 road. I slept through it all but was taken to see the craters and we brought home a piece of shrapnel.

At the beginning of August 1945, after VE Day, my

grandmother decided she would like to visit her sister and other relatives in Gloucester, as she had not seen them since before the war, and she took me with her. We had been there about a week when we were woken in the middle of the night with revellers in the street outside. It was VJ Day! We had a telegram from home telling us to come back as soon as possible as there were to be celebrations in the village.

We returned the next day and when we walked into our kitchen we could not believe our eyes. There was food everywhere. All the people in the village had brought their contributions to our house, as it was central, and an outdoor party was to be held in the evening on the village green just outside. There was a marvellous array of food. People had opened tins of salmon and fruit they had been hoarding and made lots of these delicious things. Outside on the village green was a big bonfire. When it got dark the bonfire was lit and warning lamps were placed at the entrances to the village. Our piano was taken outside and my mother played for dancing in the road. Potatoes were roasted in the bonfire and everyone had a good time. Next day there were rings on the polish of the piano where beer glasses had been put down, but nobody minded because *the war was over*!' *(June Haythornthwaite, Borwick and Priest Hutton WI)*

◨ FRIENDLY PEOPLE ◨

'I was born in 1938 and we lived in the heart of London, until Hitler decided to change that. On 16th September 1940 a bomb was dropped on our house, leaving my grandparents, parents and me with nothing but a few small possessions. My father decided that my mother and I should be brought to Lancashire to live with his brother while he was in the army.

We went to live in Lea and were immediately accepted and helped by our warmhearted neighbours. When the war was over and my father came out of the army, he asked Mum if she would like to return to London but she refused – she was not going to leave these lovely Lancashire folk. *(Ann Rigby – Ashton-on-Ribble WI)*

HIGHDAYS & HOLIDAYS

MLynskey

OFF TO THE SEASIDE

How we looked forward to our visits to the seaside – whether it was a day out or a whole week's holiday.

▣ ONE WEEK'S HOLIDAY ▣

'Our annual one week's holiday was always taken at either Morecambe, Blackpool or Southport – never the East Coast, and the anticipation was almost as exciting as the holiday.

My parents had a ritual which commenced the previous Sunday evening when we would walk to Bradford station to see the large board displaying the extra trains which would run the following Saturday, the commencement of Bowling Tide. That was the name of the Bradford holiday week when all the mills and factories shut down. After deciding which train we would take, the week seemed interminable. When the great day arrived, I, not being a good traveller, felt sick before I even got on the train.

The sun always seemed to be shining when we arrived at our destination, and we made our way to our boarding house. Of course we always had to have a "recommended address" by relatives, neighbours or friends. On arrival we were shown our bedroom, our dining table, and our section of the enormous sideboard where we had to keep our bread, cakes, tinned goods etc. No fridges in those days, so perishable food had to be bought daily. I remember shopping with my mother before breakfast for the meat for the mid-day dinner. I think we bought the vegetables and pudding from the landlady. Looking back I now realize how hard those ladies worked to make a living in the season. Fancy having to cook several types of meat and maybe fish every dinner time! They would be glad they only had to brew the tea at tea and supper time, the residents supplying their own meal.

I don't ever remember a wet week. As I recall we spent all day

'Everyone seemed to have a studio photograph taken when on holiday; this one of my mother, myself and elder sister was taken at Blackpool in the early 1920s.' (Beatrice Sellers – Greenmount Village WI)

Paddling in the sea at Blackpool in 1927. (Sheila Main – Garstang WI)

outdoors, much of the time my parents occupying deckchairs which would only cost coppers for the hire. Then in the evenings we went to a show or "the pictures". A rare treat for us as my parents had a business which was open until 8 pm weeknights and 9 pm Saturdays.' *(Ruby Dickinson – Crag Bank WI)*

❖ NEVER TO BE FORGOTTEN ❖

'One of my long-lasting memories is the first time I saw the sea when I was ten years old in 1925, on a Sunday school outing to Blackpool.

A Mr J. Hodgson in the next village, Slaidburn, started a haulage business, the first in these parts. He started with one lorry carting lime and stone from the Settle quarry, and by 1925 he had two or more lorries. But what I do know, he made these day trips and outings possible by turning a lorry into a bus. It was scrubbed out spotless and then iron supports held a strong canvas hood, with canvas going round the sides and celluloid

This open-air train did a circular tour of Blackpool Promenade in 1925 for 4d. 'Everyone in those days wore some kind of headgear, even on a summer holiday.' (Eileen Bonnet – Ainsdale WI)

windows to keep out wind and rain. Iron-framed wooden benches from the Methodist chapel, Slaidburn, were lined along the bottom of the lorry, very firm and comfortable.

When we reached Blackpool it was dull and damp. I was very disappointed, I'd been looking forward to blue sea but it just looked grey and dirty. We spent the day with another family. To stay dry the two mothers decided to take us on the Big Wheel. It was great, the carriage had a fixed double seat down the middle. I'll never forget the twinge in my tummy as we got higher, or the wonderful view of Blackpool and the sea.

Later the sun began to shine so we sat on the front to eat our packed lunch. Afterwards we had a paddle in the sea and built sand castles. Then we went to the Tower Circus, a real thrill. Finally, by this time we were very hungry so the first fish and chip restaurant in we went and did they fill our plates! Lovely!

Then it was finding our lorry (cum bus) to head back home to Newton, and a walk over the fields to home after a never to be forgotten day out.

Mr Hodgson later started the first bus service in the Hodder Valley, over the fell and round by Whitewell to Clitheroe.' *(Annie Rushton, Frances Nelson – Dunsop Bridge WI)*

◧ RUNABOUTS ◧
'Until Dr Beeching axed the train which ran from Preston to Southport, many families would buy "runabout" tickets to be used during the summer holidays, when for a comparatively small sum one was able to travel as far north as Bowness and south to the Lancashire border, as many times as one wished during a specific period. Excursions were run by train from Southport to Blackpool each Saturday night pre-war, stopping at all stations to Preston. The cost from Hoole station was one shilling return – with an extra sixpence for admission to Blackpool Tower!' *(Hoole WI)*

ALL THROUGH THE YEAR

There were high days to be looked forward to each year, including Pancake Day and May Day, and there were also those special royal occasions we all celebrated.

◧ SHROVE TUESDAY – PANCAKE DAY ◧
'One of my earliest memories of Granny, in the 1930s when I was four or five, was on Pancake Days. We would walk the half mile to her home down Whitehorse Lane, at Barton. The living room had a big matt-black and steel range with a glowing fire behind a big brass fireguard. Granny would be waiting in her rocking chair with a jug of batter, lemons and sugar bowl on the table beside her.

She was a tiny woman, already in her mid-seventies, with a deeply wrinkled face but still black hair in a tight bun. Her black skirt almost reached her black clogs with their shiny brass toe caps and studs. For cooking she wore an enormous starched white apron.

After greeting us she put the big cast-iron frying pan on the hob over the fire and plates to warm in the fireside oven. Her sinewy little wrists never failed to toss the half-cooked pancake and when it was finished she would deftly slide it on to a plate and offer it to one of us with a twinkling face. "If tha's not eten that bi time next un's ready, I'll black thi face wi't goose feathers." This was the wing saved from the Christmas plucking and used to brush the soot from the flue.

Of course this thrilling fate never befell the younger grandchildren. We were packed off home with an orange each. But after work Dad would wash and change, eat his tea, then mount his old bike and pedal off for "One of mi mother's pancakes", and I'm sure he came home with a dirty face!' *(Irene Gregson – Cabus WI)*

'In the 1940s and 1950s, Pancake Day at Brook House, Inskip, meant many young lads called for a pancake, but before dining they had to pull a pin out of the crown of a bowler hat – with their teeth! Before they arrived Granny Porter had rubbed the bowler with soot from the fire range and the lads ate their pancakes with blackened faces.' *(Pat Ascroft – Broughton WI)*

'Shrove Tuesday was always a holiday at Whitechapel (Goosnargh) school. Children would go from house to house equipped with large cloth bags. The housewife on whom they called would be greeted with "Please a pancake", and each child would be given an orange, or a halfpenny when the supply of oranges ran out. At one farm the request was taken literally and the party of half a dozen children were sat down at the big kitchen table and regaled with pancakes.' *(Jennett Fowler – Ulnes Walton WI)*

▣ EASTER AND PACE-EGGING ▣

'Around Easter, at Overton and Middleton in the 1930s, we would go pace-egging. I remember one year putting on a dress inside out and covering my face with flour – it was then the custom to go round knocking on doors and be given decorated hard boiled eggs. We used to take little milk cans round the hedges collecting gorse flowers for my mother to colour our own home-produced eggs.' *(Myra Sturzaker – Caton WI)*

'At Preston in the 1920s, on Easter Monday children took small baskets of dyed hard boiled eggs and oranges into the park. The eggs were rolled down a hill and then eaten if fit – this was our pace-egging. The boiled eggs, dyed purple or red, might have the child's name written on the shell. Avenham Park would be crowded on the day, when a band played and stalls sold brandy snaps and sweets.' *(Sheila Main – Garstang WI)*

'At Easter the pace-eggers were out on the streets performing the traditional play. Most boys took part at some time and although nothing was written down, the words were passed down and religiously learned. A shout of, "I am St George of Old England fame" early on Good Friday morning heralded their performance. It was usual for the grammar school boys to put on a more elaborate performance at the Town Hall each year but I think the motley crews who gave a free show in the streets were enjoyed just as much, as long as they kept to the traditional words and actions. Home-made swords and shields were their props, with costumes made from old dresses and pieces of curtain that had seen better days.' *(Greta Shepherd – Hornby WI)*

◼ MAY DAY ◼

'For weeks before May Day, the girls in our triangle of streets in Failsworth went through the intense ritual of preparing our maypole and its attendants. First, we chose our May Queen, whose role was to hold the maypole while we danced and sang around it. The downside of this honour was that she had to sing a solo at the crucial point of the proceedings. The strain of this ordeal led to many a last-minute mysterious illness, and the Queen first chosen was seldom the one on the day. The song was hardly Grand Opera, and went as follows:

"I am the Queen, the Queen of May,
Please listen to my song today"

I cannot remember ever being chosen as May Queen, but I certainly was brought on as substitute on several occasions as a matter of dire emergency.

After the Queen, the next grave concern was the colour scheme for our costumes, which were made out of crepe paper. If you have ever tried to make gathered skirts and boleros from this very temperamental material, you will understand the frequent tears and despair at last-minute disasters.

In the early evening of May Day, we set off around all the houses on our patch, going through our routine of "In and out the woods of bluebells" and "My mother said that I never should, Play with the gypsies in the wood, "and other doubtless deeply pagan folk memories.

We wound the ribbons round the maypole, and then unwound them, but as the ribbons were also made of crepe paper this required a great deal of skill. By the time we were halfway round, keeping skirts, boleros and ribbons intact was a very precarious operation indeed.

As each house where we performed usually contained relatives of one of our number, we collected enough money to pay a visit to Mrs Wiggins' chip shop at the end of the street. We would sit in her back-room to eat our chips and peas, and drink cherryade, Tizer or dandelion and burdock.

On a fine May evening, I can still recall the taste of the best fish and chips in the Northern Union, and the feeling that we were really living the high life! I wonder why fish and chips never taste as good today?' *(Audrey Shallcross – High Bentham WI)*

'May Day was a special day because that was when we organised our May Queen. I would beg my gran for anything to dress up in – lace curtains, old hats, anything was welcome. We would all collect in the back street to pick the Queen. This was done by tiny squares of paper, numbered and placed in one of the lads' caps. There was a great deal of shaking up and fingers crossed as we drew out our number. Alas, the magic number 1 was never mine; I was always the train bearer. However, I was in demand for the dressing up bit because I could cadge quite well and always had plenty of finery to hand out.

Then we got ready, which believe me took a considerable time due to our mums' demands – ie to mind the baby, run an errand, hold the pegs while the washing got pegged out in the back street, hold the jug as the farmer measured our daily pint from the churn in the back of his cart, and then the horse had to have his tit bits and be petted. Well, now it was time! Someone was sent to knock on the doors and our mothers brought out the best chair and put it at the side of the front door, sitting there anticipating the show and glad of a sit down, admiring one another's steps all newly scrubbed and snowy white.

Their offspring, proud as Punch, paraded up one side of the street and down the other, then all over again for the love of it. The lads had joined in, of course. They had blackened their faces with the soot from the chimney back and had on their dads' caps and scarves and were carrying their handiwork, old cocoa tins wrapped around with string to hold the contributions we were hoping for.

To round the day off we all clattered to the corner shop to spend our coppers. First of all was the lucky bag, then the rest was spent on various sweets. The lucky bag was again the centre of much excitement because we once again drew the numbers out of the cap and the one that drew the magic number 1 got the lucky bag!

Ah well, another May Day gone and all the finery returned. Funny thing about those days; the sun was always shining and life was fine.' *(Norah Shakeshaft – Little Lever WI)*

▣ ROSE QUEEN ▣

'Every summer at Parkbridge in the 1930s we had a Rose Queen festival. A platform was erected in the grounds of the big house and the ceremony was watched by all the villagers. Each queen had her retinue of six train-bearers (girls) and two cushion-bearer (boys), who carried the crowns on velvet cushions. There were coconut shies, football kicking games, races, and a housey-

Rose Queen Gladys Draper at Parkbridge in 1933. (Mavis Defley – Fairbottom WI)

housey stall operated by Frank Yates wearing his silk hat. We finished off with tea in the schoolroom, starting with the hymn *Be Present at Our Table, Lord* and waiting for grace to be said by the vicar before we dared to start eating. It all ended when war broke out in 1939.' *(Mavis Defley – Fairbottom WI)*

'The biggest event in Crag Bank in the 1950s took place in July, when the new Rose Queen was crowned, attended by her ladies in waiting and her page boy. Then came the judging of the fancy dress, in which all the villagers joined. Dads were there to organise the sports, and big and little ones ran as many events as they could to win pennies. Afterwards came tea, with sandwiches, jelly, ice cream, tea and lemonade. All the mothers had worked hard the night before preparing the food and arranging tables and seating in the village hall.' *(Joan Woodhouse – Crag Bank WI)*

Happy faces at Crag Bank in the 1950s at the judging of the fancy dress. (Joan Woodhouse – Crag Bank WI)

▨ CHRISTMAS AND NEW YEAR ▨

'For 50 years, Catforth Womens' Institute organised a children's Christmas party. It was the highlight of the Christmas period. Children walked two by two along the road to the school (partners were chosen from the opposite sex and were seen as an indication of who you intended marrying in about 20 years time!). A'Hunting We Will Go was a regular, and we took about an hour to play, while everyone had their turn to gallop down the room with their partner. Then came the tremendous knock on the front door of the hall, and legs went to jelly and littles hearts pounded as Father Christmas was welcomed in.' *(Pat Ascroft – Broughton WI)*

'On New Year's Day the strains of Longridge Prize Band could be heard across the fields as they came out to the country district round about. First footing was taken seriously in some households and pains were taken to see that a dark man was the first to cross the threshold in the New Year. One woman who had ensured that the dark-haired postman would be the first caller

Longridge Brass Band c1930. 'My father rejoined the band in the 1960s and one of his first engagements was at a Club Day in Cleveleys in July, when they walked about six miles in serge uniforms and he was acting as stand-in on the big drum.' (Mary Headley – Caton WI)

was foiled when she answered her door and two little red-headed boys ran in to ask her sons to come out to play. No particularly bad luck followed!' *(Jennett Fowler – Ulnes Walton WI)*

▨ CORONATION DAY ▨

'At the time of the 1937 Coronation of George VI, I was only three years old. There was a fancy dress parade at Priest Hutton and I was dressed as a Lyon's "nippy" (waitresses from the Lyon's Corner Houses must have been popular at the time!). Everyone in the village seemed to have dressed up and even the babies' prams were decorated. This was followed by sports and a tea in the Memorial Hall. The children in the village were all given a Coronation mug and I still have mine.

In 1953, when our present Queen was crowned, we had just bought our first television set and were anxious to see the Coronation. We invited some neighbours who had not yet acquired a set. In the afternoon, events in the village followed a

Fancy dress at Priest Hutton Coronation celebrations in May 1937. (June Haythornthwaite – Borwick and Priest Hutton WI)

similar pattern to 1937, with fancy dress, sports and a tea. The school added three extra days to the Whit Week holiday. A week after the Coronation the school was closed for the day and the children were taken to the Palace Cinema in Lancaster to watch the film *Elizabeth is Queen*, and some of the children also went to see a film called *A Queen Is Crowned* at the Roxy in Carnforth. The children all received a Coronation mug from the school, too.' *(June Haythornthwaite – Borwick and Priest Hutton WI)*

'Our family had planned to listen to the 1953 Coronation on the radio, but to our delight our neighbours, who had the only television in the neighbourhood, invited us in to watch the ceremony on their nine-inch black and white set. We were so excited we descended on them after breakfast and stayed there until the evening.' *(Val McGlynn – Withnell Fold WI)*

WHITSUNTIDE AND WALKING DAYS

Whitsun was a very special time of the year, and Walking Days were big occasions in town and village alike.

▣ FAILSWORTH WHIT WALKS ▣

'The highlight of the summer in our area of south Lancashire was the Whitsun Walk, or Procession of Witness to give its proper name. Different religious persuasions had their preferred days – as I remember, Catholics in Manchester walked on Whit Monday, Protestants by and large on Sunday or Friday.

Failsworth, where I was born and grew up, lies between Manchester and Oldham, and was a fiercely independent Urban district before the war. Its religious bias also was strongly Nonconformist. Although it boasted two parish churches and a Catholic church, there were at least six assorted Nonconformist chapels, with full houses every week, and thriving Sunday schools. When I was a child between the wars, the two parish churches did not join in the big walk on Whit Friday. We always understood that the schism had been caused by St John's, the "top" parish church, maintaining that they should lead the procession every year because they were the established church. The chapels, however, took it in turns to be leaders. That way, everyone had their chance to be behind the band, and no one was allowed to get above themselves. It was not until after the Second World War that the parish churches gave up the struggle and became as equal as everyone else! The spirit of our "long-nosed Puritan" forefathers was alive and flourishing in our neck of the woods.

But long before the great day arrived, there were meetings of mothers and Sunday school teachers to discuss the really important details – whether the girls would carry bouquets or baskets of flowers, what kind and colour, real or artificial – a crucial consideration given that it could rain. For the bigger girls,

WHIT-SUNDAY, MAY 24th, 1953.

PROGRAMME OF

United Sing and Procession

of the following Failsworth Sunday Schools :

1—Failsworth Methodist Church.
2—Macedonia Congregational Church.
3—Church Street Mission Church.
4—New Jerusalem Church (Swedenborgian).
5—St. John's Parish Church.
6—Roman Road Independent Methodist Church.
7—Holy Trinity Church.
8—Bethel Methodist Church.

The Schools all meet on Wrigley Head Green at 2-30 p.m. prompt. After singing the hymns, the procession, headed by the Brindle Subscription Prize Band, will proceed along Wrigley Head to Ellesmere Street. Then down Oldham Road to Bethel Church, where all Schools, except Bethel Church and Holy Trinity Church, will return along Oldham Road to their respective Schools. Bethel Church will proceed along Oldham Road to Broadway, and then return to their own School. Holy Trinity Church will return to their own School via Linwood Street, Hobson Street and Poplar Street.

The Knutsford and Cross Town Silver Prize Band will lead the third School.

St. Bartholomew's Prize Band, Wilmslow, will lead the fifth School.

The Preston Town Silver Band will lead the seventh School.

President : Rev. A. LEES, B.A.

Procession Marshall : Mr. N. GRAY.

Secretary : Mr. K. LEECH,
21, Ellesmere Street, Failsworth.

The programme for Failsworth's Whit Walks in 1953. (Audrey Shallcross – High Bentham WI)

the pinnacle was reached in Class 4 at ten to eleven years of age. That year you carried the strings of the embroidered banner which preceded each church. All these girls wore long dresses of the same material and supposedly the same style. However, since they were all made by various local dressmakers, mothers or aunties, the interpretation could be fairly loose. There was another perk to this honour. Until you grew out of the dress you were roped in as bridesmaid by any member of the family, however distant, who had a wedding in the offing.

When the Second World War broke out, I was due to carry the bannerstring in the summer of 1940, and I could hardly believe that anyone could be so heartless as to deprive my class of this prize. However, as my mother had already bought the material – Swiss-embroidered organdie – my aunt made up the dress and it did service at several wartime weddings.

For all children, this was when you had your new "best" clothes for the year, and wore them for the first time on the Walk. Before leaving for Sunday school on Whit Friday, we went round to friends and relations who slipped a penny into our pockets for luck. When we left the house, we were warned what would happen to us if we stopped to play on the way and spoiled our pristine appearance.

There were many anxious moments, rising to fever pitch by Whit Friday, all centred on the weather. Amongst the most anxious were the young men who had to carry the banner poles, who prayed fervently for a windless day. If there was a solid downpour, the Walk could be postponed to the following Sunday, but somehow that was never the same. There was a real problem in this case if the girls' flowers had been real, hence the agonising over real versus artificial. The worst scenario was showers – there is something very uninspiring about a procession under umbrellas! There were also drawbacks even on a hot and sunny day. Most of the girls wore white buckskin shoes, and no matter how many dire warnings our mothers issued, it was very hard to resist poking a toe into the tar puddles. The result was a sorry mess and a heap of trouble.

But nothing could match the excitement of the Walk itself – the bands, the crowds, the Wesleyan Boy Scouts' drums and bugles suddenly blasting forth, and everyone casting a critical eye over members of other Sunday schools as the procession did a U-turn and we passed each other. We ended up very tired and sticky, but with a wonderful glow as we relaxed and changed into our play clothes in the evening.

When I married and went to live in other parts of the country, I was amazed to find that Whitsuntide was scarcely recognised even as a religious festival. Now Whitsun is not even a holiday, and the magic has gone.' *(Audrey Shallcross – High Bentham WI)*

◈ MANCHESTER WALKS ◈

'On the great day itself, Whit Monday for the Protestants, Whit Friday for the Catholics, we were up with the lark. Hopeful that the sun would shine – and to my mind now, it always did – we were too excited to eat and were bathed with hair brushed and shining, ready long before time.

From the suburbs of Manchester they came in their hundreds. Each church had their banners, depicting the name of the church, St James, St Barnabas, Christ Church and so on, at the top of the banner and the district at the bottom. It was no mean feat carrying these, especially if there was a breeze.

It was such a gathering, such a chattering, laughing host, with a few tears from young ones for one reason or another, a chaotic mix that somehow got sorted out into orderly groups ready for the procession. Like flocks of exotic birds, we girls were in every conceivable colour, complemented by the more sombre shades of the males, all in our Sunday best. Pennies and ha'pennies were placed for safety in pockets or purses, coins given by relatives and friends, admirers of the little peacocks.

Everyone waited for the man with the big bass drum. At last, strapped into his leather harness, the drum supported on the front of his body, he was ready. Musicians in place, instruments gleaming, peaked caps pulled straight, musical scores fixed upon their supports on the instruments, the signal was given. With a grand flourish of the drumsticks, the man struck the drum ... boom de boom, de boom boom boom! Then up spoke the trumpets, the cornets, the trombones and all the instruments of the big brass band.

Feet began to tingle with the urge to move as the stirring martial music of Sousa poured out, then the parade moved off, slowly at first, gaining confidence until everyone moved in unison.

Men and women of Ukrainian descent, wearing national dress, walked each year at Bury after the Second World War. (Lillian Zurowskys – Cockey Moor WI)

On we marched to the centre of the city, to Albert Square. School after school, church after church, a long snake of many colours and darker hues, each headed by its own brass band. Smiling people lined the route, cheering us on, waving paper mops, flags, celuloid windmills twirling round and round. They enjoyed the spectacle and the music, for as one band faded into the distance another one was coming by.

When we reached the Square, tired but happy, the mass of people, both walkers and spectators, filled it. Vendors milled amongst the crowds, selling sweets, ice cream, flags and balloons and I still recall with affection the paper Japanese sunshade which was bought for me.

A service was given, hymns sung, voices swelling up to the high heavens in harmony. At last we were disbanded. The demand for pop and tea was terrific. Lyons Café and other tea

217

'Outside my parents' shop in North Road, Preston in 1907. The Whitsuntide processions were a big occasion in the Preston calendar, with crowds lining the streets six deep and chairs placed along the front and upstairs windows at a premium. The three markets in the town were covered with swings and roundabouts, and hot potato and parched pea stalls, and there were performing fleas, fat ladies and Tip the Mermaid Out of Bed!' (Sheila Main – Garstang WI)

shops did a roaring trade. When eventually our hunger and thirst were appeased, pennies spent on what appealed at the moment, we assembled for the homeward journey.

Although we strode out valiantly, the journey did seem longer. White shoes would become spotted by the tar that oozed out of the stone sets with the heat of the sun, forming bubbles, which proved irresistible and had to be popped.

The band played us on, back to our base, encouraging us, and now with hindsight I admire their stamina. Imagine carrying an instrument and playing it more or less continuously for several miles and many hours. Youngsters were met by their parents and eventually we dispersed to our homes. The walk was over for another year. Over half a century later, I can remember it well.' *(May Forrester – Overton & District WI)*

WHIT SUNDAY AT ASTLEY

'Our church walked on Whit Sunday and it was a day we looked forward to for weeks, hoping it was going to be fine. New white dresses (never coloured), our hair put into long rags to make ringlets the night before, and praying that the blue irises would be out in flower for Mother to decorate our walking baskets.

During the week we would go to neighbouring towns to watch churches who walked their parishes, but Whit Sunday was always special. Our Sunday school would hire a barge which had been scrubbed out clean and with our mothers and fathers, all the Sunday school children, teachers and church people, we would sail to Lymm down the Bridgwater Canal. It took a long time and we would arrive about dinner time at a farm which was on the side of the canal. On arrival we all lined up for a glass of fresh milk, then went to the village school to have a picnic meal which the teachers had brought with them. During the afternoon we played games and had sports races in the field, parents joining in. I remember my Mam and Dad winning the three-legged race. More sandwiches for tea and then we would sail home. I never remember getting home; we were soon fast asleep.' *(Betty Bailey – Astley WI)*

WE ALL WALKED AT WESTHOUGHTON

'I grew up in the little Lancashire cotton town of Westhoughton. The parish church is St Bartholemew's but it is a sprawling parish and apart from the Sunday school held in the Parochial School next to the church there are three other Sunday schools – Hart Common, Chequersbent and ours, White Horse.

One of the highlights of the church year came in June: Walking Day, a procession of witness similar to the Whit Walks. Every group in the church walked: the Mothers' Union, the Church of England Men's Society, the Guides, Scouts, Cubs and Brownies, the choir (in their robes), the churchwardens, the curate and the vicar. And every member of the Sunday school walked, from the Superintendent to the tiniest child.

Each Sunday school had a large banner suspended between wooden poles which were carried in leather holders over the

The Whit Friday Walk in 1952 with members of Greenmount Congregational Church. (Beatrice Sellers – Greenmount Village WI)

shoulders of young men, former Sunday school pupils. White Horse's banner depicted Christ seated, His hand raised in blessing with the words "Suffer the little children to come unto Me". Older boys held on to the three ropes attached to each pole to help keep the banner upright on windy days and about two dozen ribbons were attached to the back and front of each banner. The ends of the ribbons were carried by the girls in matching dresses.

Each Sunday school had a brass band and it was with great excitement that we at White Horse listened for the distant sounds of the bands as Hart Common walked to the parish church and then they and the Parochial School walked in procession to White Horse, as did Chequerbent from the other direction. Then, together with four bands and four banners, we all walked in a long procession to the parish church and on to a nearby field for tea and a little talk from the vicar, followed by games and races.

For the rest of the year or until outgrown those dresses were known as our "walking dresses".' *(Joan Burgess – Ainsdale WI)*

INDEX

LIST OF CONTRIBUTING INSTITUTES

Contributions have been received from the following Lancashire
Women's Institutes

Abbeystead ● Ainsdale ● Appley Bridge ● Ashton-on-Ribble
Aspull and Haigh ● Astley ● Aughton Moss ● Banks ● Belmont
Blacko ● Bolton-by-Bowland ● Bolton-le-Sands
Borwick and Priest Hutton ● Bradshaw and Harwood
Broughton ● Cabus ● Calder Vale ● Caton ● Chipping
Claughton-on-Brock ● Clayton-le-Dale ● Clayton-le-Woods
Cockey Moor ● Crag Bank ● Crank ● Cronton ● Dunsop Bridge
Eccleston ● Fairbottom ● Garstang
Goosnargh and Whittingham ● Great Harwood & District
Greenmount Village ● Hapton ● High Bentham
Higher Walton ● Hoghton ● Hoole ● Hornby
Hurst Green ● Kirkland ● Ladybridge ● Lathom
Leck and Cowan Bridge ● Little Lever ● Little Mitton and District
Little Thornton ● Livesey ● Longridge ● Longton ● Lostock Hall
Lund ● Lytham Green ● Mawdesley ● Mere Brow and District
Moss Side ● Nether Kellet ● Over Kellet ● Overton and District
Pendleton ● Rufford ● Sabden ● St. Annes-on-Sea
St. Michael's-on-Wyre ● Scarisbrick ● Shevington
Simonstone with Read ● Slaidburn ● Staining
Stalmine with Steynall ● Stoneclough ● Thurnham,
Trawden and Winewall ● Ulnes Walton ● Warton ● Weeton
Wennington and District ● Whitechapel and Inglewhite
Winmarleigh ● Withnell Fold